Turn on the light on science

A research-based guide to break down popular stereotypes about science and scientists

Antonio Tintori and Rossella Palomba

]u[

ubiquity press
London

Published by
Ubiquity Press Ltd.
6 Windmill Street
London W1T 2JB
www.ubiquitypress.com

First published 2017

Cover design by Amber MacKay
Images used in the cover design are licensed under CC0 Public Domain.
Main cover image: skeeze / Pixabay
Background cover image: Freepik

Printed in the UK by Lightning Source Ltd.
Print and digital versions typeset by Siliconchips Services Ltd.

ISBN (Paperback): 978-1-911529-04-0
ISBN (PDF): 978-1-911529-05-7
ISBN (EPUB): 978-1-911529-06-4
ISBN (Mobi/Kindle): 978-1-911529-07-1
DOI: https://doi.org/10.5334/bba

The full text of this book has been peer-reviewed to ensure high academic standards. For full review policies, see http://www.ubiquitypress.com/

Suggested citation:
Tintori, A. and Palomba, R. 2017. *Turn on the light on science: A research-based guide to break down popular stereotypes about science and scientists*. London: Ubiquity Press. DOI: https://doi. org/10.5334/bba. License: CC BY 4.0

To read the free, open access version of this book online, visit https://doi.org/10.5334/bba or scan this QR code with your mobile device:

Contents

Acknowledgements

Aside from our own efforts, the success of *Light'13*, the project that is at the heart of this book, largely depended on the support and encouragement of many others. We take this opportunity to express our gratitude to all the people who have been instrumental in its successful completion – we felt motivated and encouraged by colleagues, and without their encouragement this book would not have materialized.

The activities on which this book is based were financially supported by the European Commission under the Marie Skłodowska-Curie Actions programme. This support was vital to the implementation of the *Light'13* project. The publication of this Open Access book has been funded by the European Commission FP7 Post-Grant Open Access Pilot.

We are very grateful to Ana Muñoz van den Eynde and Stephen Roberts for their insightful comments during the peer-review process.

Antonio Tintori
Rossella Palomba

Both authors share responsibility for the content of this book. Antonio Tintori wrote Chapters 1 and 4; Rossella Palomba wrote Chapters 2 and 3 and the introduction. The conclusion was written jointly.

Light: a project, a format, a method, an event

Rossella Palomba

Do you hold stereotypes? If you answer "No" to this question, then you probably do hold a lot, and use them all the time, without knowing it. Stereotyping is a fundamental process of the human mind through which our brain can easily stock a large amount of information; it involves oversimplification and overgeneralization, because you apply to all the members of a group the characteristics that you have learned to associate to that group either by meeting one or a few of its members or from parents, peers, the internet or the media.

There are three main reasons why nobody is free from stereotyping: stereotyping is efficient from a cognitive point of view, because you no longer need information about an individual

How to cite this book chapter:
Palomba, R 2017 Introduction. *Light*: a project, a format, a method, an event. In: Tintori, A and Palomba, R. *Turn on the light on science*, Pp. vii–xvi. London: Ubiquity Press. DOI: https://doi.org/10.5334/bba.a. License: CC-BY 4.0

if you are aware that he or she is a member of a specific group; and it is reassuring, because you feel better about yourself, in the case where you hold pejorative attitudes towards those who are different.

As noted by Kahneman, we have two modes of thinking: the fast mode and the slow mode. The fast mode operates automatically and quickly, with little or no effort and no sense of voluntary control; the slow mode allocates attention to the effortful mental activities that demand it and to situations where you are asked to do something that does not come naturally. Because you have a limited amount of attention that you can allocate to the various activities, actions, tasks or problems that fill up your life, stereotyping represents an automatic easy reaction to a complex world (Kahneman 2011).

You stereotype people every time you are unable to obtain and/ or understand all of the information needed to make a reasonable judgement about them, their professions, or their goals. Many authors (see for example Ramirez-Berg 2002; Sosnizkij 2003; and Ndom, Elegbeleye and Williams 2008) have observed that in the absence of the so-called "total picture", stereotyping the members of groups allows you to fill in the missing pieces of information.

Breaking down stereotypes that are established over time – and possibly reinforced by the media and internet – is not an easy task. Part of it involves becoming conscious of holding these stereotypes: if you are aware of your hidden biases, you can monitor and attempt to change your attitudes. It may not be possible to avoid the automatic stereotype or prejudice, but it is certainly possible to consciously amend it. In situations in which information about a particular target group is clear, relevant and highly informative, the stereotypes we hold also mean much less and become irrelevant. On the other hand, when personally obtained information is absent, or is ambiguous, people do rely on the stereotypes they hold. Obviously the problem of stereotype removal cannot be solved by simply explaining that your attitudes are based on a wrong image of reality: no matter what we say, you will be inclined to hold your beliefs intact.

Bearing this in mind, we can raise the second and – for this book – more relevant question: do you stereotype scientists? Here you will probably answer: "Don't know", or "I never thought about it". You are not the only one who never considered the possibility of holding stereotypes about scientists and their work. Scientists themselves rarely think about it: often they do not care about the potentially biased image people have of them, or simply do not make any effort in conveying the correct image of their profession because "it is not their task".

If one asks scientists why they decided to embark on a scientific career, they will most probably answer that it is a privilege to be immersed in a world as stimulating as science is, or that they like dedicating their life trying to understand how the world works. By answering in this way, they perpetuate and reinforce the stereotype that scientists are somehow "different" from ordinary people – and anyone who is different, is immediately suspect.

Contrary to what is the case with many other professions such as those of medical doctors, pharmacists or lawyers, one very rarely has the chance to meet a real, flesh-and-blood scientist. As reported by Deloitte (2015), in the EU-28 there are 1.63 million researchers (in Full Time Equivalent), who account for less than 0.7 per cent of the total labour force. In other words, the chance to meet one of them or to have a scientist among your group of friends or neighbours, unless you are yourself a scientist, is very low. This makes it very difficult for you to review your ideas about scientists, to become conscious of your own biases, and to move beyond them.

The world is increasingly reliant on science, and yet a large portion of the general public has a wrong image of scientists and their work. We are all aware that science is taking quick steps forwards, that scientific results have an immediate and tremendous impact on our daily lives, and that the future is closer than we imagined. Therefore it very relevant for our societies that the image of those who produce this fantastic progress, i.e. scientists, be positive, attractive, inspiring and unbiased. Changing the public image of scientists, closing the gap between science and the wider society and developing new and simpler ways to communicate science produces a deeper consciousness of the relevance of science for our societies and a growing attractiveness towards scientific jobs.

Since 2005 the European Commission has committed itself "*to enhance* [the] *public recognition of researchers and their work*". The tool identified for achieving that goal was the organization of the European event called Researchers' Night, held during the same night in many European towns. The main objective of this action was "*to bring researchers closer to the larger public, with a view to enhancing their important role in society, and in particular within the daily life of citizens*" (European Commission 2007b, p. 25).

Every year, the European Commission launches a call for proposals under the framework of the Marie Skłodowska-Curie Actions programme in order to give funds for the organization of Researchers' Nights all over Europe. In the annual calls for proposals for the Researchers' Nights, stereotypes and the possibility to tackle them was mentioned among the expected impacts; we therefore immediately understood the importance of such events for testing our ideas on how to let people break down the stereotypes they hold about scientists.

In answering the call for proposals, the basic idea of many organizers of the Researchers' Nights held around Europe is that science is so rich and has such deep content that putting scientists on stage and letting them talk or do funny experiments with people is enough to leave the attendees enchanted by science and scientists. This idea is true, but do people change their opinion about scientists? Do they break down the stereotype that researchers are highly gifted individuals, smart geniuses, with superior abilities to reason, generalize or problem-solve, and somehow above everyone?

Our project, called *Light: Turn on the light on science* (hereafter *Light*), had exactly the aim of undoing the stereotypes about scientists; it consisted of a big field test carried out in Italy that involved more than 100,000 people over several years. In this book we present the results of the 2013 edition of *Light* (*Light'13*), which was our last proposal funded by the European Commission (we started in 2008) and the final outcome of six years of testing, adjusting and confirming hypotheses on how it is possible to undo the stereotypes concerning scientists and their work.

This book is not just about organizing events: we wanted to change the stereotype of a scientist. In order to comply with the European Commission's rules about Researchers' Night, we had to do so during a science communication event, and our event, which took place over a few hours and in one location, attracted 15,000 people. This is different from organizing a talk with a scientist at a school or a science café, with a limited number of people discussing with researchers.

There was no doubt that between the two fundamental models used in science communication, i.e. "deficit" or "dialogue" approaches, we had to choose the latter. In fact, in the deficit approach the audience members are assumed to lack the necessary knowledge about scientific concepts, and therefore communication goes from scientists to the public, reinforcing the idea that scientists are special people who work on things that "*you people wouldn't believe*", just to quote from the famous movie *Blade Runner* (1982). Conversely, in the dialogue approach there is a two-way exchange of information between scientists and the public: scientists have scientific facts and experience at their disposal and the members of the public have personal interests in the scientific experiments presented.

But is simple interaction enough to let people catch a glimpse of the human side of a scientist? Can the dialogue between scientists and the public go beyond an enthusiasm for science and result in a change in attitudes towards scientists? Interaction and dialogue are necessary but not sufficient conditions for obtaining such a change.

To reach our goal, we started by drawing a list of the most common images people have of scientists, mainly conveyed by TV series or movies. For example, if we talk about a chemist you probably picture a middle-aged male, wearing a white lab coat and mixing up strange liquids in strange glass bottles. And a physicist may be a guy who looks like Einstein, with no social skills, playing with risky equipment all the time. In the first chapter of this book, through a review of recent literature, you will be equipped with all the necessary information on the most common stereotypical images of scientists, held by ordinary people. Results from surveys carried out at IRPPS-Research Institute on Population and Social Policies and in similar institutions will also be presented.

In order to let people abandon the idea that scientists are dispassionate geniuses, somehow above ordinary people, we thought that the first step should be to remove any barrier, material or psychological, that could impede a fluent and real interaction between scientists and the public. The set-up of a location can have a tremendous impact on people's emotions and attitudes. Such impact has been analysed and studied to create friendly working environments, for example, but very few social scientists have paid attention to architecture and design with a view to remove the communication barriers that are built up between the public and researchers simply by using the materials at disposal (desks, chairs, microphones etc.).

We started a partnership with architects and designers in order to create an innovative set-up of the location where we wanted the public to meet researchers. 'The *Light: Turn on the light on science'* project was a consortium of two partners: the Italian National Research Council (CNR) and Triplan Ltd, a private architecture, design and communication firm. Architects working in the public realm are continually collaborating with experts to enable a design to be transferred from paper to a fully functioning scheme. We transferred that method to stereotypes' removal. At the conceptual stage, we exchanged ideas and opinions and discussed the possibilities offered by existing materials, with the objective of getting the architects to design a package that responded to our need of undoing the stereotypes about scientists and that at the same time made for an attractive environment for users.

Additionally, in order to let the public catch a glimpse of the human side of researchers, we created a special entertainment space called the Globe Science Theatre where scientists performing arts or doing sports entertained the public. The aim was to show what a scientist does when a scientist is not doing science and overall to demonstrate that scientists do have hobbies, that some of them do these hobbies in a very professional way and that none of them spend all their time trapped in their labs.

Finally, we created specific activities aimed at addressing the gender stereotypes affecting the situation of women in science. In our experience, talks, data, role models' speeches, posters or exhibits have no permanent effect on people's minds. Gender stereotypes are very deeply rooted and even female scientists do not fully understand how much gender bias informs the decision-making and behaviour in their scientific labs or institutions. Our collaboration with the architects was crucial in this respect: we organized a number of sensory experiences where people could have a first-hand experience of gender differences in science through their own senses, i.e. by participating and not just by listening or watching.

The set-up of the event mentioned above will be described and explained in greater detail in Chapter 2. We will also include a list of practical suggestions resulting from our experience. In reading it, you will learn what we did and how you might re-create the conditions to make people review their opinions about and attitudes towards researchers.

As observed by Bultitude (2011), one crucial factor when working with groups from the general public is that the groups are not homogeneous: each person has his or her own interests, prejudices and concerns. Among all possible subgroups of the so-called "general public", we were particularly interested in changing the attitudes towards scientists of young people in order to let them embark on a scientific career. Specific activities were set up based on a peer-to-peer interaction between young inventors, who were students still going to school, and young people in general, in order for them to develop the self-confidence needed to get into science, engineering and technology and to turn it into a "cool" career. We organized a national competition inspired by the television music competition *The X Factor*. The difference was in content: no music, but creativity and inventions realized at school. Chapter 3 deals with this aspect of the project and gives some practical suggestions about how to replicate the initiative.

The final chapter presents the results of surveys we did among people participating in our events and the evaluation of their change of opinions about researchers through the activities we presented.

This book presents a research-based guide on how to break down stereotypes about scientists and science. It is intended for a wide audience with no formal training in science or engineering. Our intention is to raise awareness of how stereotypes affect people's image of scientists and science and help people self-correct, and thereby reduce the negative effects of stereotypes on people's minds. Stakeholders and managers of scientific institutions, who are increasingly conscious of the relevance of communicating research results directly to the greater public and want to overcome the cultural barriers existing between scientists and laypeople, may also find new ideas in this book. Our work may also be of help to educators seeking to protect themselves against negative stereotypes about science careers, to adopt a growth mindset in encouraging students' life aspirations and choices in the fields of Science, Technology, Engineering and Mathematics (hereafter STEM) and to combat gender stereotypes. Finally, the book should also appeal to scientists looking for ways to better their communication skills, and invites them to reflect on the negative impact of a strict "academic" behaviour on the general public and young people in particular. A self-evaluation is therapeutic from time to time to correct behaviour and communicate scientific results to the greater public correctly.

Now is a good time to expand opportunities for scientists and non-scientists to interact and understand each other in formal, non-formal and informal settings. In 2014, the European Commission launched a new seven-year strategy on Responsible Research and Innovation (RRI), a cross-cutting issue of the new framework programme Horizon 2020. As stated by the European Commission (n. d.), the objective of RRI is "*to build effective cooperation between science and society, to recruit new talent for science and to pair scientific excellence with social awareness and responsibility*". In light of this new European vision, stereotypical images of scientists and science should be removed and there is a need to find practical solutions to facilitate the dialogue between scientists and citizens.

This book is a step forward in this direction. Perhaps it is the right book at the right time to make at least a small difference in suggesting how we can change people's minds towards scientists and their work. But let us be frank from the start: there is no one recipe for removing stereotypes about scientists. In this book we will present the path we followed, as what we did can help to better understand what kinds of activism are likely to be effective.

CHAPTER I

The most common stereotypes about science and scientists: what scholars know

Antonio Tintori

1.1 When Illusion Becomes Reality

Each of us has a biased world view because we are all limited to our personal perspective on reality. We can only see what is before us, we can only hear what is around us and we can only recognize, order and process what we have seen, read or heard about before. It is useful to categorize reality because it allows us to manage large blocks of information concerning complex social elements. Who will ever have the opportunity (and take the time) to gain first-hand knowledge of all the aspects of the surrounding reality, i.e. the different kinds of individuals and facts, or the

How to cite this book chapter:
Tintori, A 2017 The most common stereotypes about science and scientists: what scholars know. In: Tintori, A and Palomba, R. *Turn on the light on science*, Pp. 1–18. London: Ubiquity Press. DOI: https://doi.org/10.5334/bba.b. License: CC-BY 4.0

whole variety of social groups? Stereotypes help us in the complex task of simplifying our world by sorting everyone and everything into tidy categories. It is an abstract but clear and simple mental process.

In his work on the theory of social identity, Tajfel highlighted the close relationship between simplification and distortion of reality. Stereotypes are basically generalizations concerning social groups, aimed at binding the cognitive process to the cultural context. In order to do that, stereotypes emphasize and overestimate the characteristics of a social group that make it different from the others (Tajfel 1974).

Among the stereotypes concerning scientists, there are those considering scientists a group of clever, bright, reserved, socially clumsy people, devoted only to their work – all characteristics that make them different from ordinary people. Altogether, these images convey the message that scientists are somehow "different" from ordinary citizens. Needless to say that this is a stereotypical image of scientists, developed and simplified within our social and cultural context; an image conveyed and continuously reinforced in the mass media or based on reputations passed on by parents, peers and other influential agents of socialization.

Stereotypes give us a standard idea of the world that is very easy to understand; they organize a standard reality that resists criticism. As observed by Lippmann (1991), stereotypes are the products of cultural and groups' ideas, play the role of categorizing social elements and in the majority of cases produce inaccurate and biased social judgements, whose incorrectness would be impossible to verify. Even when the validity of a stereotype is verifiable (for example when you meet a scientist who in his or her free time is a chef, or a musician, or a keen sportsperson), this first-hand knowledge does not contribute to the stereotype's refutation, and you will continue to hold it unless you perceive positive effects of the stereotype's removal on your personal situation or on your social group.

A stereotype is a rigid perspective on the world. It is based on bias. It represents beliefs that are not necessarily negative but certainly irrational, and may result in very negative attitudes and behaviours, as for example in the case of racism and xenophobia. Stereotypes are also potentially dangerous because they may generate judgements that are not based on first-hand experience.

A typical stereotype concerning scientists held by ordinary people is that scientists are responsible for many environmental catastrophes (think for example about the Fukushima Daiichi nuclear disaster on the 11th March 2011) and consequently that they are irresponsible people, willing to sacrifice everything in order to make experiments or lacking concern for the consequences of their actions – a very damaging stereotype that may make citizens more suspicious of scientists and less supportive of the policies that scientists personify.

Bourdieu (1998) speaks of *hidden persuasion*, which shows up in different forms of socially recognized aestheticism; a form of "symbolic violence" that is transmitted with culture, limiting personal freedom and our cognitive horizon. The order of things and the abstract characteristics of social groups are examples of social persuasion, supporting stereotypes (Bourdieu 1998). A good example are gender stereotypes within science, which influence the image of scientists and their career developments.

From childhood, individuals are exposed to cultural biases concerning their role in society. These biases generate beliefs that are deep-rooted and difficult to break because they reflect a wide social consensus, and which contribute to the creation of expectations concerning appropriate life choices on the basis of the sex of the individuals. As noted by Tintori (2015), people inherit gender stereotypical ideas as *reality* – a *generalist reality*, based on the "natural" roles of men and women in society.

Science is considered a masculine world and the so-called "ivory tower" remains a male dominated place. A superficial look at the national, European or international statistics on researchers broken down by sex is enough to understand that there is a clear prevalence of men in senior and leadership positions. Merton speaks about a *self-fulfilling prophecy*, when individuals perceive cultural norms as obvious and prescriptive (Merton 1948). According to Tintori (2013), women are considered unsuitable for science because of their main – "natural" – role as family caregivers, which cannot be combined with work as challenging as science. Thus, women and mothers are more likely to join the ranks of the second tier, or to drop out of academia and scientific labs, perpetuating the stereotype that science should be a men-only profession (Tintori 2013).

1.2 Is The Frankenstein Myth Still Alive?

The most common stereotype of scientists held by many adults evokes a smart, hard-working, eccentric, workaholic man. The image conveys an idea of social isolation and of an "unbalanced" life, without family and children, friends, hobbies or interests. It also implies someone who is socially ill at ease, with limited interpersonal skills and a tendency to see things in black and white based on the data, and sometimes misanthropic and often sexist. It is to be noted that many people perceive scientists not (or not mainly) as working for the good of humankind but rather for personal gain. Why this image? There are many reasons for this.

We create stereotypes to explain why things are the way they are. As Dovidio (2009) notes, stereotypes do not have to be true to serve their purpose. The world would be chaotic if we changed our attitudes towards people too easily (Dovidio 2009). Thus, stereotypes typically evolve slowly, often becoming more complex and nuanced over time. This is the real strength of stereotypes and explains why attempts to suppress them may actually cause them to return later, stronger than ever.

Ordinary people have scarcely any opportunities to develop a personal view of scientists and their work by coming into contact with them. First-hand experiences with scientists you "know in passing" (i.e. someone you may see and interact with on an occasional or even regular basis, as in the case of neighbours) are not enough to dislodge stereotypes about the whole category, because these occasions may be considered discordant experiences or exceptions to the rule set by cultural stereotypes.

In Europe the image of scientists still takes pessimistic forms. The special Eurobarometer survey carried out in 2010 with results published in 2015 showed that a majority of European citizens (62 per cent of respondents at the EU-27 level) feel that science can sometimes damage people's ethical sense, and 53 per cent feel that scientists are too powerful and potentially dangerous. Overall, the Eurobarometer survey shows that European citizens are positive about science and technology, but over time there has been a slight shift towards scepticism compared to the 2005 survey. Although science may bring benefits, Europeans do not have too high hopes that science and technology can solve all the world's problems. Furthermore, the survey shows that the public on the whole has become less sensitive to issues about science and technology, less enthusiastic about the potential benefits and less concerned about the potential drawbacks (Eurobarometer 2015).

Since the 19th century, the master narrative of the scientist has been one of a crazy, reckless, extravagant, sometimes dangerous man. Mary Shelley's *Frankenstein* provided an imagery and a vocabulary universally invoked in relation to scientific discoveries and technological innovation that have greatly contributed to create negative stereotypes about scientists. Written by Shelley in 1818, the novel tells the story of Victor, a man obsessed with the unlimited possibilities of modern science, and therefore contemptuous of ethical rules and of the social implication of his behaviour. In this narrative, knowledge leads to the temptation to "play God", interferes with "nature" and determines who lives and dies.

Nowadays, the image of scientists conveyed in the media is often that of individuals motivated by unacceptable scientific curiosity, who become drunk with the power of knowledge, disregarding the consequences of their discoveries. *Dr. Strangelove* (1964), by Stanley Kubrick, is a famous movie that describes the events that could have happened if a mentally deranged American general had ordered a nuclear attack on the Soviet Union. Dr Strangelove is the US President's science advisor, and is a lunatic scientist whose arguments about nuclear weapons and the need of a nuclear attack are perfectly rational. The movie was released a few years after the Cuban Missile Crisis, one of the most critical moments of the Cold War: this is a clear demonstration that the stereotypical "mad scientists" tend to be working on whatever the public is afraid of at the moment, and it is interesting to see how interests in science shift with society's fears.

From Mary Shelley's day to our own, most scientists, and biomedical scientists in particular, have shown strong moral consciences: far and away they save lives, rather than threatening them. But the Frankenstein myth never dies. Turney (1998) demonstrated that

Mary Shelley's classic novel and the myth it spawned have provided images that have been incorporated into popular debates about advances in biology, from the debates of the early 19th century to the contemporary concern over genetic engineering.

Many people acquire their perception of the Frankenstein myth solely through experiencing popular media. In the media the image of dangerous scientists re-emerges with any new discovery that appears to threaten the social or natural equilibrium. Haynes has argued that in Western literature and culture "*Victor Frankenstein is alive and well*" (Haynes 2003 p. 245). Poisons developed by industrial chemists, genetically modified fruits and vegetables, nuclear risks, the danger represented by hackers, and the cloning of the embryos of mice and of sheep – and in the future perhaps of children – create fear of the power and change that science entails, leaving many people feeling confused and disempowered.

Jurassic Park (Crichton 1990) was not the first sci-fi novel (and film) to deal with genetic tampering, but it presented fictional cloning experiments on dinosaurs' genes with a high degree of realistic scientific detail. Crichton's story finds its predecessors in books like *Frankenstein* and H.G. Wells' *The Island of Doctor Moreau* (1896) and their film adaptations; the technological details are different, but the essential idea is identical: the modern fear of genetic modification. Movies did not invent that fear, but have merely given it shape, perpetuating the idea that we cannot abandon our role as creatures to become creators, and that having the scientific ability and skills does not imply the right to do so.

The scientist described, according to Haynes (2003), as an evil and dangerous man is an easy subject for writers and filmmakers, a convenient shorthand for the simplification of the narrative; in the wider public, however, it generates confusion and a feeling of helplessness in relation to the ethical themes that people feel close to (Haynes 2003). Scientific power is often enveloped in a shroud of mystery that gives it an dark charm. For example, *Star Wars*, the epic space opera created by George Lucas, is a great metaphor of the risk of uncontrolled scientific progress. Science and technology should be driven by the moral imperative to advance knowledge, avoiding any supposed supremacy of scientific authority.

The stereotype of scientists as clever, but untrustworthy or insane, people has generated negative feelings towards the scientific profession. Odifreddi (2012) speaks of a double misunderstanding concerning scientists and their attitude towards everyday problems. On the one hand, scientists are seen as individuals with wandering minds who are often out of touch with reality; on the other hand, this lack of "conformity" is seen as an emotional disorder, because our culture worships attention and we assume that the best behaviour is to stay focused on issues and problems (Odifreddi 2012). The truth is that you can be a nonconformist individual without being crazy, as well as being a scientist without being a genius focused on your work all day long (this is in fact closer to the normal state of affairs!).

As observed by Chambers (1983), alchemy and black magic were invoked for centuries by caricaturists with the aim of making fun of chemists. This *"image has been cleaned up and, in a sense, standardized"* (Chambers 1983, p. 255). Some years later, Eugster (2007) observed that the stereotypical image persists and scientists continue to have image problems. A bad image hurts scientists on many levels: administrators allocating research funding may be swayed by a poor image; young people with a poor view of scientists may be dissuaded from pursuing science as a career; and, finally, the general public, which interacts with technology every day, may have little or no idea about who is working to create the science behind that technology.

Movies and television are important cultural factors, and reach both adults and children. Frayling (2005) wrote a comprehensive paper on how scientists are depicted in movies and he contrasted the scientist's image from the first half of the century with that from more recent movies. He argued that, recently, scientists in the movies have become "mavericks", often fighting against the government or some unidentified institution. This "maverick" image is no better than the "mad scientist" one, and the reason is that both stereotypes are inaccurate (Frayling 2005). This makes changing perceptions of scientists really important, because if the main image of scientists is of older, white men with glasses in lab coats, girls and boys are not going to imagine themselves as scientists.

1.3 The Good, The Geek And The Ugly

A long line of studies show that the words we use affect the way we think. Language pervades social life; it is the main vehicle for the transmission of cultural knowledge, and the primary means by which we gain access to the content of others' minds. Language is implicated in attitude change, social perception, personal identity, social interaction, intergroup bias and stereotyping, and so on. It is a powerful indicator of underlying cultural values and, among other things, it is a powerful tool in maintaining and reinforcing stereotypes about science and scientists. In fact, stereotypes are not fixed and do change over time through social transmission of information, similarly to the way in which language evolves.

Dikmenli (2010) conducted an interesting qualitative survey of stereotypes among undergraduates using a free word-association test regarding science and scientists. Words associated with scientists included both negative and positive descriptions, and fit into various categories: personal characteristics, activities, work-places, technological developments and physical characteristics. Following Mead and Métraux (1957), who carried out one of the first and most influential study of stereotypes of scientists, stereotypes were identified as either "positive" characteristics (e.g. smart, highly trained, hard-working) or "negative" ones (e.g. dull, geek, nerd, dork). Each of these words generates different images in people's minds, images which are likely to come from a mix of characters seen in popular television and film.

Many stereotypes about scientists have arisen alongside the evolution of the word *geek*, an evolution which relies on the depiction of scientists in movies and television and is fostered in the collective and popular culture. As observed by Cross (2005), the term *geek* describes someone who is more intelligent than average and works outside the mainstream or behaves in a non-normative way. It is similar to the word *otaku* in Japan, which is used to tag people as addicted and isolated, and obsessed by manga (Japanese comics and cartooning).

In the past two decades, the word *geek* has evolved significantly and become almost synonymous with *nerd*, another term for awkward outsiders. In mainstream media portrayals the stereotypical nerd is, with few exceptions, depicted as male, white and enthusiastic about mathematics, computer science and technology (see for example Kendall 1999; Bucholtz 1999; Eglash 2002; Woo 2012; Quail 2011; Robinson 2014). *Nerd* also means a kind of lone wolf, reluctant to socialize. Though not interchangeable, the geek and nerd characters are somewhat indistinguishable from one another when it comes to their depiction in popular culture. However the terms are used, the words *geeks* and particularly *nerds* have an intrinsic negative connotation and speak to the "otherness" of the subjects in question.

Geek and nerd scientists are passionate about science and technology. This characteristic is not negative per se: we are all attracted by scientific discoveries and the advancements of science, and we all value curiosity and intelligence. But when the passion for science becomes an obsessive one and scientists are so personally committed to their research that they forego families, friends or romantic relationships, then the stereotype of geek scientists sends us back the image of a socially deviant individual.

A number of negative traits are often associated with the nerd/geek image: poor hygiene or posture, glasses with thick lenses and people always working at personal computers or using some sort of sophisticated technology. According to Mercier, Barron and O'Connor (2006), greasy hair and thick black glasses are images mostly associated with nerds and geeks, while unattractive, pale, thin, spectacled individuals are associated with computer scientists.

It is also a safe bet that the majority of these images are of males. As noted by Leon (2014), the very absence of female images of which to get rid of is a clear demonstration of the fact that female geeks or nerds either do not exist in the media, or exist in such a minority that they hardly merit mention. The few depictions of these women that are seen in popular culture are often merely a feminized version of their male counterpart, and still incorporate, and perhaps even amplify, negative traits such as those mentioned above (Leon 2014).

The modern-day detectives and scientists seen more and more frequently on prime-time television are geek men and women. Even within a single show like *Criminal Minds* (2005), there is a marked difference between the "good-looking" and "clever" field agent Dr Spencer Reid and Special Agent Penelope Garcia, the quirky, brainy and bespectacled woman always seated at her computer desk. The TV show *NCIS* (2009) also offers a contrasted image between the well dressed and intuitive Special Agent Leroy Jethro Gibbs and the Forensic Specialist Abigail "Abby" Sciuto, who prefers to work alone on the computer, wearing tight pants and platform boots.

Inaccurate portrayals of men and women in science reinforce negative stereotypes about geeks, and also reinforce negative stereotypes about gender, to the point where sexism may be considered "normal" within the context of the geek and nerd community: girls cannot be into "nerdy" things because nerdy things are about science, strategy and action, which are inherently male. The rare instances where people admit that female nerds do actually exist are almost always in media representations that paint women as unattractive people, incapable to show emotions; stereotypical "feminine" traits such as beauty, fashion, social skills and sexual desirability are depicted as at odds with "male-nerd-only" traits such as intelligence, technical mastery and supposed lack of sexual desirability.

The depiction of women as incompatible with nerdiness has real-world consequences, as shown in Tocci's ethnographic studies (Tocci 2007). When women are exposed to "nerdy-white-guy" stereotypes, they are strongly discouraged from entering STEM fields; stereotypes associated with that particular scientific field are often incompatible with the way girls see themselves and can steer women away from that field.

Stereotypes influence the life choices of girls, keep women out of science careers and stop women at the lower levels of the scientific hierarchy. Indeed there are females playing STEM-literate characters that are gaining more popularity in the movies or in television series; for example, Sandra Bullock stars in *Gravity* (2013) as a female astronaut or Emily Deschanel plays

Dr Temperance Brennan, who is the forensic anthropologist protagonist in the television series *Bones* (2005). But the female scientist is still an atypical image and women are being held back by stereotypes. Geek, otaku or nerd, fans of math, technology and other sciences: we always speak of very smart people, isolated, obsessive – and male.

Over the past two decades, the most positive stereotype of the scientist as hero has appeared with increasing frequency as a central character both in film and on television. This trend towards more positive images does not mean that scientists are portrayed realistically. As the communication researchers Nisbet and Dudo noted in their synthesis of studies of on-screen scientists, *"whether a nerd, a villain, or a hero, each of these archetypes are not reflective of scientists generally as a profession or as citizens"* (Nisbet and Dudo 2013, p. 242).

The recent trend has been towards presenting scientists as heroes and warriors of science; the longstanding idea that the entertainment industry produces only negative stereotypes of scientists (i.e. the "mad scientist", Dr Frankenstein, the geek) is now weakening. Nisbet and Dudo (2013) made examples of positive images that include Dr Alan Grant as the main protagonist in the *Jurassic Park* films; Spock in the 2009 version of *Star Trek*, who takes on leading-man and action-hero qualities to rival Captain Kirk, or the recent movie *The Martian* (2015), where an astronaut who was mistakenly presumed dead and left behind on Mars uses his scientific skills in his struggle to survive.

First and foremost, positive stereotyping is still stereotyping. In other words, positive stereotyping affirms the perception that scientists are different based on their exceptional skills and abilities and has the capacity to be just as damaging as the negative form of stereotyping.

The European Commission and other international and national institutions are trying to improve the image of science and scientists, but the influence of these stereotypical media stories is still very strong and takes us away from the real science. The reason may lie in the fact that the real science is still too far removed from the general public.

1.4 Why Public Perception of Science Matters

Over time, increasing attention has been given to the so-called "popularization" of science. As Hilgartner (1990) has noted, the popularization of science rests on a two-stage model: first, scientists develop genuine knowledge; second, science communicators spread polished versions of it to the public. At best, popularization is seen as a low-status task of "appropriate" simplification of scientific results, and creates knowledge gaps between real and popular science. Most popular of all, of course, is the image of eccentric academics pursuing their research with scant regard for practical matters, cut off from the rest of society in their ivory tower. The atomic bomb, genetically modified food and the extraction of stem cells from human embryos are just some of the developments that people see as having a morally dark side; as a consequence, science might not necessarily look like it is for the good of all.

As observed by Marnell (2012), the truth is that, whichever sub-discipline you consider, science is a difficult subject. Its concepts are mostly abstract ("what are gravitational waves?"), its discoveries often counter-intuitive ("how can black holes collide?") and the mathematics needed to describe its discoveries are sometimes barely understood even by university-trained mathematicians ("what are the mathematics of topology?"). This all makes popularizing science a difficult task: make it too simple and it will inspire few; make it too difficult and nobody will be interested in it.

The difficulty of understanding the relevance of scientific discoveries and their social impact negatively affects the image of scientists. In Europe, the problem of public recognition of scientists and science persists, and the European Commission takes initiatives to change attitudes towards science and scientists. Recently we (the authors of this book) were guests in the laboratories of the National Institute for Nuclear Physics, a research centre in Frascati, a few kilometres south of Rome. During the visit a colleague showed us an historical and very important instrument: the Electron Synchrotron. Fascinated by the gigantic object, we asked what it was for. We received the following answer: "It was of no use". We later learned that the Electro-Synchrotron was an important tool for experiments in the field of particle physics: the machine was a very important particle accelerator, since the 1960s it had enabled significant scientific advances and it is fundamental for the study of electromagnetic properties. So it must have been of some use!

Our experience demonstrates that the gap between scientific activities and communication exists. In other words, even when the progress of science might have important and positive impacts on the quality of life of citizens, these successes are not often understood by the public, because of inadequate communication. We are convinced that science should not be only for scientists, because is too important: it is the way in which we explore the natural and social world and it is the dominant – and currently the only legitimate – form of human knowledge. For the good of society, the public and scientific progress itself, science needs a broader community and its results should be communicated to the wider public in a correct and engaging way. This idea has moved us to organize big scientific communication events to dismantle the stereotypes about science and scientists, as described in the following chapters of this book. The economic support of the European Commission was essential.

After visiting Frascati, we tried to get information on the Electro-Synchrotron; would we have done the same without our scientific curiosity? We should probably have thought the machine was something extremely expensive but useless. Often, it is difficult to understand what the practical use of scientific research might be, whether the research consists in sending a rover to Mars, exploring the genetics of fruit flies or making particles collide. However, it is vital that the processes and products of science are readily available for the public to understand and interrogate, because the stereotype of the useless science with scientists cloistered in their ivory towers of knowledge relies on the lack of appropriate communication. Scientists are considered people who think in a way that is qualitatively different from "normal" people, and therefore they are often seen as entirely rational, objective and very smart. This paints science as a near-infallible institution that does not want or require engagement from non-scientists.

A major influence on everyone's perception of science is of course the media. Television and the other mass media do more than simply entertain and provide news. They confer status on those individuals, groups and issues selected for placement in the public eye, indicating who and what is important. Those made visible through the mass media become worthy of public attention and concern; those whom media ignore remain invisible. Therefore, mass media are a relevant tool to channel a positive image of scientists; this is also even more relevant if scientists are broadcasted at prime time or on TV news programmes with a large audience.

Scientists have a crucial role in making scientific findings accessible to the media, and thus to the public. Obviously scientists should know how to communicate advances in their fields, but they should also be given consideration and be able to get a fraction of the media's attention. Important discoveries are not enough to transform scientists into communicators or to make people listen when scientists speak.

Physicists, chemists, palaeontologists or historians, for example, do not feed people's appetite for the novel and extraordinary (which leads to media coverage) as space exploration or advances in medicine do. When these types of scientists have the chance of getting media attention, they often fail in communicating their findings because they try to educate the members of the public rather than to engage with them, and maybe because deep inside these scientists consider it "unprofessional" to explain what they do. Thus, they appear either "too smart" or out of touch with the "real world", generally messing around with chemicals or scribbling notes in lab books. We tried to dismantle these stereotypes through specific outreach activities involving scientists and non-scientists, because as long as people believe that scientific careers are for passionate geniuses only, many boys and girls might not personally identify with those stereotypes or find them relevant to their life and career choices.

Scientists have much to contribute to society, and they have the right and responsibility to do so. The dialogue between science and the rest of society has never been more important. The Europe 2020 strategy makes clear the need for public recognition of science and scientists. As observed by Geoghegan-Quinn, former European Commissioner for Research, Science and Innovation, to overcome the current economic crisis we need to create a smarter, greener economy, where our prosperity will come from research and innovation. Science is the basis for a better future and the bedrock of a knowledge-based society and a healthy economy (Geoghegan-Quinn 2012).

The stereotypes of scientists (smart, isolated in their ivory tower, focused on their work, crazy, evil and dangerous) are hard to dismantle if there is a lack of discourse and contacts between scientists and the non-scientific public. Of course, there will always be stereotypes in the media, but, ideally, through smarter engagement with the public the positive images of scientists should outweigh the negative ones. The majority of scientists are intelligent, passionate, dedicated, entertaining people, and it is possible to change the narrative about scientists and science, to let people understand who scientists are and what they do and to finally dispel the stereotypes about scientists.

CHAPTER 2

How to undo stereotypes about scientists and science

Rossella Palomba

2.1 Change Is Not Easy

Stereotypes are easy to create. The experiences we have and the socio-cultural environment in which we are immersed provide all the necessary circumstances to create stereotypes with little mental effort on our part. We are accustomed to categorize and to generalize about the qualities of the categories we create, we are made to be receptive to socio-cultural inputs, and not to question our experiences. But even if you understand fully how you bring stereotypes in, you might not be willing to kick them out. In fact, as observed by Schneider (2004, p. 364), *"beliefs about groups*

How to cite this book chapter:
Palomba, R 2017 How to undo stereotypes about scientists and science.
   In: Tintori, A and Palomba, R. *Turn on the light on science*, Pp. 19–49. London: Ubiquity Press. DOI: https://doi.org/10.5334/bba.c. License:
   CC-BY 4.0

of people are likely to be learned as a part of a cognitive package that includes beliefs about political, religious, and cultural matters. Therefore, stereotypes are going to be easier for you to learn (and probably harder to disavow), just because they have many connections to everything else in your mind".

This does not mean that you should consider stereotypical thinking as unavoidable and succumb to the worst of it. But you need to understand that the process of undoing stereotypes is not easy and that it should respond to some criteria, which we are going to illustrate below.

In the previous chapter we learned a lot about stereotypes concerning science and scientists. We know that a "Professor" brings to mind the image of an individual who is highly intelligent, yet socially inept; excels in the academic world, yet fails miserably in the realm of common sense; and is completely immersed in complicated experiments and processes, and busy round the clock. The idea of a scientific lab is that of a misogynist place where men are the dominant sex, full of obscure and complicated apparatus, where in some extreme cases unhinged men perform dangerous experiments. In some cases there is the idea that science is not meant for the progress of humankind but just for satisfying the curiosity and sense of power of elitist individuals.

If we want to undo stereotypes about science and scientists we should start with some basic assumptions, as observed by Schneider (2004). First, stereotypes are generally false, because of the limited experiences you have with people coming from a group you do not know well, as in the case of scientists. Often, television, movies, newspapers and magazines convey stereotypical images of what a scientist is or should be and people do not have any possibility to check the validity of this stereotypic thinking.

Second, if we want to dislodge stereotypical images of scientists, we assume that experiences, contacts and interactions with real scientists should provide clear evidence that disconfirms the stereotypes. Casual contacts with one or more scientists are ineffective, because people may consider them to be atypical individuals of the category (see Hewstone 1994; McClendon 1974; Rothbart 1996). Suppose you hold the stereotype that philosophers are boring and pedantic, and that at a party you meet one who is a lively and amusing person: will this count as evidence disconfirming your stereotype? Do you start thinking that philosophers are quite friendly people? You will actually probably decide that this person you have met is an atypical philosopher and you will place this person in a special category with only one member: the person you met, an exception to the rule. Therefore, the context in which you meet scientists, the quality of the contacts and the interactions you have with them, as well as the duration of the interaction, are fundamental aspects affecting the rejection of stereotypes.

Finally, we assume that, when people recognize that their own stereotypes are false, they will be willing to change them. This last point is a relevant aspect in the process of undoing stereotypes. Hodson and Hewstone (2013, p.83) have argued that *"there is substantial evidence that creating awareness of social categories during contacts, either by making categories explicitly salient or by presenting representative out-group members, can lead to generalized attitude change"*. In other words, if you are conscious that you are interacting with a group of scientists that show qualities and behaviour very different from the stereotypical images you hold, this will provide you with sufficient information to change your beliefs and attitudes about scientists as a group. Following Craik (2008), we add that, if the contacts and interactions take place between the social group you are a member of (i.e. your group of friends, family, colleagues, classmates etc.) and the "out-group" (in this case, scientists), you will be encouraged in changing your attitudes if the whole group of people you belong to has the same reaction.

In brief, in order to undo stereotypes about scientists and science we need: contacts and interactions between scientists and ordinary people, in a favourable context, and where you are not isolated from the social groups to which you belong.

Given the aim of undoing stereotypes about scientists and science, we should define which stereotypes we intend to undo, how we want to undo them and when and where to undertake this activity. Within the framework of a project funded by the European Commission called *Light: Turn on the light on science*, we decided to tackle the most popular stereotypes about scientists. In order to be consistent with the idea that groups of people, rather than isolated individuals, should be exposed to the activity of disconfirming stereotypes, we organized big events under the European Commission Researchers' Night "action". This gave us the possibility of verifying the validity of our activities on large numbers of people. The activities we implemented were designed to reach out to everyone – not only to "science addicts". Families with children and people of any age, but young people in particular, participated in our communication events.

Among the stereotypes affecting science and scientists, we decided to tackle the following: that scientists are impersonal individuals, ready to act as "oracles" from their ivory tower of knowledge; that they are solely interested in satisfying their curiosity to discover the truth; that they are especially gifted individuals, different from "normal" people; that scientists should be men, and that science is not for women; and that scientists do nothing but work, and never have fun.

Special attention was given to gender stereotypes in science. We know that the image of a scholar is mainly that of a middle-aged man. Some of the elements of this stereotype are certainly true, because women are still under-represented in many areas of STEM and are a minority at the top of the hierarchies of academic and scientific institutions.

The unconscious bias penalizing women in science because of their gender should be overcome because it is a matter of equity as well as the fact that part of society's investment on education would be wasted. Bearing this in mind, we decided to deal with gender stereotypes in science in the following ways: on the one hand we wanted to demonstrate that women are as good as men in all fields of science; on the other hand we wanted people to experience what it means to be a woman working in scientific research, going through the difficulties women are faced with because of the gender structure of the research system.

2.2 Dismantling The Ivory Tower

When scientists are portrayed in movies and television, they are often shown isolated in laboratories, alone with their complicated apparatus, sometimes with a big blackboard filled with equations behind them. This can make science look like a solitary exploration of the world and give the wrong impression of scientists trapped working in their laboratories, detached from reality. This is especially true when scientists are interviewed by journalists during television news broadcasts, mainly to explain natural catastrophes, virus epidemics, food contamination and other alarming events. On these occasions, scientists provide the "experts' interpretation" of reality. This is not bad per se, but the image conveyed in this way to the general public is far from positive, because it reinforces the stereotype that researchers are somehow cold individuals removed from the messiness of real life.

As a matter of fact, scientists work in busy labs, surrounded by other scientists and students. They often collaborate on studies with other scientists all around the world, and even the rare scientist who works entirely alone depends on interactions with the rest of the scientific community to scrutinize his or her work and get ideas for new studies. Nevertheless, it is true that, over the centuries, science has become institutionalized, with solid structural boundaries separating professional scientists from ordinary people.

In order to dismantle the stereotype that scientists are elitists who refuse to leave the comfortable confines of their ivory towers, we should bring the labs to the people. We are convinced that the opposite, i.e. bringing people into scientific labs to see how scientists work, is not fully effective in breaking down stereotypes about scientists and might have unwanted side effects on people's minds. When you enter an environment that you do not know and do not understand completely, your first reaction is a mix of awe and disorientation. Even if you feel curiosity and interest about the topic, lab visits are not enough to overcome feelings of being intimidated by complicated and obscure matters, and more often than not the idea that scientists are super-gifted isolated people remains unaffected.

On the contrary, however, visiting labs and learning more about science is an important activity for young children, because the stereotypes we learn as children influence the attitudes, beliefs and social expectations about science and scientists we later hold as adults. A long line of studies – see for example van Tuij and Walma van der Molen (2016); Bandura et al. (2001); Gottfredson (1981) – show that stereotypes play a relevant role in shaping children's occupational aspirations and choices, especially for girls.

When stereotypes are deep-rooted in the minds of adults, they cannot be dismantled simply through visiting labs and looking at scientists as if they were museum pieces. As long as science is carried out in windowless buildings and the front door requires a badge, it is inevitable that the stereotypes surrounding the ivory tower remain an insurmountable barrier and the public continues to regard academics as out of touch or distant.

There are many ways to connect scientists to ordinary people. A very popular way is the organization of Cafés Scientifiques. The founder of Café Scientifique was Duncan Dallas, and the first Café was held in Leeds in 1998. Cafés Scientifiques take place in casual settings such as pubs and coffeehouses, are open to everyone and feature an engaging conversation with a scientist about a particular topic.

Since 1998, the Cafés have spread across the world: around 300 Cafés, adapted to different cultures and audiences, are now established in 40 countries. Some countries have also established Junior Cafés in schools to promote youth engagement with science. Café Scientifique, Science Café, Science Exchange, Caffèscienza, Chai and Why, STEM Café, Wissenschafts-Café, Science in the Pub are all names indicating the possibility for a variety of audiences to meet face-to-face with local researchers. It is surprising that an initiative from a city in the north of England aimed at connecting academic research to the public has spread around the world so rapidly. We know that science can no longer rely solely on government support, and that it needs the support of the public as well. Ranganathan (2013) has issued the following call: "*Scientists: do outreach or your science dies*". Thus, Cafés Scientifiques are a step forward in bringing together scientists and the general public in a friendly environment and are a good start to break down the stereotype of the ivory tower.

The Cafés Scientifiques vary in size, frequency, number of science speakers and choice of food and drinks, but they must all comply with an unwritten protocol: the expert must introduce the topic and then the microphone is offered to the public for questions. As observed by Grand (2012), in the organization of Science Cafés there is now a tendency towards applying the academic, themed conference format. There are Cafés where the audience sits neatly in rows, the speaker stands behind a table (sometimes with a lectern), slides of bullet point notes are projected and members of the audience use a microphone to ask questions one at a time. The warm and friendly atmosphere of a discussion in a coffeehouse or pub may therefore disappear and the goal of sending friendly signals from the ivory tower may fail to be achieved.

Cafés Scientifiques were the first attempt to create a direct contact between scientists and ordinary people; many others followed over time and came to life in a range of different places: schools (primary or secondary), universities, leisure centres, museums, local public halls, public squares and natural sites, just to name a few. In Europe, every year, the European Commission gives out funds to organize the Researchers' Night, which takes place in more than 300 European cities and is a very popular science communication event.

When you decide to organize a science week, a science festival, a Researchers' Night or any science communication event conducted outdoors, it should be clear in your mind that the target audience of different initiatives is not the same, because it depends on the venue, which plays an important role. For example, if you organize a science outreach event at a university campus, your target audience will be probably be high school students, teachers and maybe families with children, and the activities will consequently be aimed at stimulating public knowledge and excitement for the disciplines represented in the university departments. In the case of a science fair or festival in a public space, you will be faced with a diverse audience of non-experts with different interests and levels of attention.

If your objective is to dismantle the stereotype that scientists are cloistered within the academic ivory tower, by definition your activity should take place outside the walls of science centres, research institutions or university campuses. In our experience, the venue is extremely important both for attracting people and for the effectiveness of your action, which is aimed at breaking down the stereotype that scientists are shut off inside their labs. The venue should have high usability and accessibility by car, bus or underground; have a good capacity in terms of number of visitors to be hosted; and be attractive per se. The last point is extremely important.

Our *Light* science communication event managed to attract 15,000 to 20,000 visitors per location in a limited number of hours. The venues were the Museum of Roman Civilization and the Planetarium in Rome, the Botanic Garden in Palermo, the Museum of the Present in Rende, Cosenza, and the headquarters of the offices of the Province of Benevento, located in a medieval fortress. The public was attracted by the science communication activities, by the presence of many scientists available to talk with the public and by the opportunity to visit sites that are generally closed to the public or need a paid ticket to be visited. The objective of undoing stereotypes about scientists and science was not openly communicated to the public, but it was the final goal of the Researchers' Night we were organizing.

In our experience streets or squares are not suitable places for changing people's minds towards scientists and science. Obviously streets or squares are by definition outdoor places, but people who come to interact with scientists at the booths you place along the street or in the square are not really interested in listening to, or entering into dialogue with researchers. Some of them will be, but the majority will be people passing by for different reasons, just stopping for a few moments by curiosity and then immediately forgetting the message you are delivering. It is important that people be exposed to the activities you organize for a time of on average one and a half to two hours in order for the activities to have some effect on the stereotype you intend to dismantle. If scientists interact with the general public for too brief a period of time, we are just treading water and not making any significant breakthrough with the change of people's beliefs and misconceptions. The members of the public should be receptive and prepared to become captivated by the marvellous things scientists are doing and as a result be ready to change their opinion about researchers. Otherwise, you are wasting time and money.

Once you have selected the venue, you have a crucial problem to solve: how to create a real two-way communication between scientists and the public. This is not a trivial issue, because, despite a general agreement among science communicators that the top-down model of "teaching people science" is inappropriate, there are still many scientists who operate in this way when communicating their results.

As observed by Jenkinson, Sain and Bishop (2005), the messages you deliver should be meaningful, in order to have the expected positive effects, but the derived meaning might differ from the intended one. The unity of meaning can be improved through two-way communication, bearing in mind that any change encounters an initial degree of resistance and can only happen if people believe that they (individually and/or collectively) will benefit from it (Jenkinson, Sain and Bishop 2005). Therefore, real two-way communication is essential for making sure that your message has been correctly received.

The majority of communication events or occasions for scientists to meet and explain to ordinary people what they are doing continue to use the academic style. Also, when hands-on activities are organized, the "deficit model" is implicitly present, because there is no willingness to overcome the material and psychological barriers between experts and non-experts.

Scientists and ordinary people are like strangers to each other: they have never met before (or very rarely), they are not able to understand each other's language, and they are driven by different goals, values and interests. Nevertheless, they can enter into a dialogue and have profitable communication, based on an interactive process of learning together. Ballantyne (2004) has argued that mutual understanding can take place even when the parties agree to differ; scientists and non-scientists are aware that they differ, and they may be willing to talk and listen to one another because of the recognized differences.

From the very beginning, we were convinced that the spatial context (i.e. the setting and design of the science communication event space) might act as a catalyst for undoing stereotypes about scientists and science, creating an agora for the potential shift in non-scientists, away from their misconceptions on scientists. In order to provide such a space, we had many meetings and profitable discussions with the event designers and architects at our project partner Triplan Ltd, who were experts in event organization and planning. We succeeded in creating a channel for reciprocal comprehension about the activities best adapted to the public and to the objective of dismantling the ivory tower stereotype, and feasible with the means at our disposal. The final setting and design of the events organized with the European Commission funds reflected this mutual understanding.

We identified three fundamental interaction characteristics that may favour the interaction between scientists and ordinary people: interaction experiences should be social, not isolating; they should touch people' s hearts and minds; and they should offer that which cannot be found elsewhere. The first two qualities depend on the setting; the third one is related to the content of the event.

We organized the event space without booths or scientists standing behind tables. Scientists and non-scientists were both protagonists of a two-way communication and exchange of opinions on different topics. There were different "corners" where people could interact with scientists; visitors could move freely from one corner to another without waiting for something to happen. When furniture was needed to support equipment such as microscopes, we favoured round tables or work desks around which people could crowd. In order to maintain a friendly exchange of opinions, no one used microphones. The experiments, discussions and hands-on activities engaged groups of people in order to avoid isolating experiences. We wanted people to feel reassured, in changing their opinion about scientists, by the fact that their friends, their family members or the visitors they might occasionally meet and talk to during the event expressed the same new feeling towards scientists and what scientists do.

A wide range of tools were used to create a welcoming atmosphere and at the same time an interactive space, after the model of a science fair. Event designers facilitated dialogue using a variety of devices to engage attendees in a way that permitted and even encouraged social interaction with scientists. For example, touchscreens were avoided, because they favour an isolated experience

Figure 1. Set-up of the event (All Rights Reserved © IRPPS-Institute for Research on Population and and Social Policies).

for visitors, while big screens were placed in every science corner so that everybody could see what was happening there and be drawn into taking part in the activity. All science corners were highly illuminated in contrast to corridors or passages, in order to capture people's attention towards the "light of science"; every science corner was identified by an attractive name and a gigantic coloured banner and backdrop that explained the content of the corner with images, as shown in Figure 1. The whole venue was purposively set up for the event, and to some extent thus became "contaminated" by science. Lights, coloured carpets and music were introduced to give it a friendly and pleasant atmosphere.

Furthermore, we did not want people to feel disoriented by being immersed in a world they did not know well and overwhelmed by many different experiments, without a clear thread linking all the activities. We are convinced that an event theme is necessary and that the choice of the theme should be made carefully.

The theme sets the general tone of the event and it lets the attendees know what they should expect from coming to it and participating in the activities you organized. It is a kind of title, broad enough to leave room for a wide range of topics. In our opinion, themes such as "Sustainability", "Imagination" or "Equilibrium", as we saw in some science festivals, are unclear for the general public and not really attractive, while other themes directly connected to academic disciplines such as "Health and medicine" or "The future of physics" are too specific and will attract only an audience interested in those disciplines.

In our events we used themes that made reference to recent facts reported on breaking news broadcasts and in newspapers. Television and other media are the major channels of information on science. From time to time, on breaking news reports scientists are invited to comment for a handful of seconds on natural catastrophes, climate changes and other alarming events. In some exceptional cases, scientists themselves make the news. This happens when researchers are called upon to illustrate the scientific advancements they achieved in specific sectors, such as new cancer treatments, the discoveries of new planets or the experimental detection of the Higgs boson. Whatever the reason for the interview, people get superficial information listening to experts' explanations on TV, and still have a lot of unanswered questions and unsatisfied curiosity.

The themes we selected for our *Light* event were "Science on breaking news" (*Light'12* theme), "What's up with science?" (*Light'13* theme) or "Real science and TV series" (*Light'11* theme). The last theme was inspired by the fact that TV series (e.g. *House, Numbers, CSI* etc.) convey an image of scientists as socially inept, downright eccentric or even completely antisocial and maverick, thus contributing to the production of a distorted image of scientists in popular culture. There is no doubt that television viewers understand that the show is fiction and that things are exaggerated or altered to suit the story; but after watching a drama with scientific content, they accept certain events as being realistic and internalize an image of researchers and their work that may be incorrect or biased.

For the activities related to the theme, you have to choose topics that fit both your theme and people's interests. We offered people many different experiences, from "creating a tornado" to "identifying your DNA". Scientists were present to explain, entertain and answer questions in a non-academic style. The "why" of the scientific discovery or experiment they were illustrating was as important as the "how", so that people could understand that what is driving scientists is not their curiosity but the achievement of social benefits for everyone. At our *Light* event, different disciplines were mixed together and several senses were engaged at the same time: vision, smell and taste. We wanted people to feel that scientists are not trapped in ivory towers and that they are very happy to engage in discussions and dialogue about their work with non-experts. We also wanted people to develop a visceral passion for the progress of science, just as we scientists have.

2.3 Scientists And The Public: Can They Talk?

When scientists talk about their research studies, they use a scientific jargon related to their discipline. As observed by Martin (1992, p. 16), jargon serves *"to police the boundaries of disciplines and specialties"*, in order to preserve the security of the academy from invasion from outsiders and to block assaults from other disciplines. But jargon serves another purpose too – it separates scientists from the so-called general public: *"Academics may battle*

among themselves over knowledge, but they have a common inter-
est in maintaining the status of academic knowledge in the eyes of
outsiders" (Martin 1992, p. 16). Thus, speaking clearly to a wide
audience might be considered a challenge to scientific status.

As a result, scientists often fail to communicate their findings
and to interact with the public. Some of them consider it "unprofessional", in the deep of their hearts, to explain what they do in
simple terms. They appear either "too smart" or "too highbrow".
Obviously nerdy scientists do exist, but there are also really "cool"
ones. The stereotype that all scientists are super-smart and nerdy
people was exactly the one we wanted to undo. This sounds easy
to do, but for many science communication events it is the greatest challenge of all.

Some years ago a press conference was held at the Italian
National Research Council (CNR) to launch a very important
science communication event, whose theme was "Horizons", i.e.,
implicitly, scientific horizons. The press conference was open to
the general public, policy-makers, stakeholders and scientists of
various disciplines, including to us, the authors of this book. The
main speaker was a scholar at the top level in the internal CNR
hierarchy and a prominent physicist. He started speaking about
unresolved physics problems, using slides full of graphs and equations. As you know, equations are dense mathematical notations,
and people are used to study equations, not to see them flashed on
a screen for one or two minutes. We came out with the impression
that the talk had no other purpose than to convince the audience
that the speaker was really smart, science really difficult and its
horizons far removed from our interests.

Though most will agree that it is important for scientists to be
able to communicate with non-scientists, this type of communication is a skill that many practising scientists lack, as observed

by Brownell, Price and Steinman (2013). There are scientists who have a natural gift for communication: they have lively personalities that help them interact with the public. Often, they are able to have empathy with the public, putting themselves in the non-experts' shoes or seeing things through non-experts' eyes. Their clarity of expression is well tuned to the public's listening capacity, maintaining high levels of attention and interest in people and at the same time having the precision of language that is needed in science: quoting a sentence attributed to Einstein, "everything should be made as simple as possible, but not simpler".

Many of the misconceptions about science that people harbour have their origins in the imprecise language used by scientists who try to be understood by those they consider as lacking the necessary knowledge. As pointed out by Bohren (2001), inadequate language weakens and distorts ideas, fails to create emotional responses in the minds of members of the audience and is easily transformed into nonsense by laypeople. It will then take years, if it ever happens, to purge misconceptions from people's minds (Bohren 2001).

While there are good communicators among scientists, there are also bad ones. Distinguished scientists may have difficulties abandoning their jargon or may have careless speech habits. Often they are convinced they are successful communicators because they are able to open their mouths and utter a stream of complicated words; they may have misconceptions about the capacity of ordinary people to understand and comment on what they are doing.

If you aim at dismantling the stereotype that scientists are somehow "different" from ordinary citizens, interaction, dialogue and reciprocal knowledge between scientists and the general public are essential. The idea is to show that scientists may be cool and friendly, and that, although immersed in a challenging and passionate professional life, they fit well into society; do not make the mistake to think that science is so rich and has so much interesting content that it is enough to let scientists talk and make experiments with the public. Sometimes this works, but in the majority of cases it does not.

For the *Light* event, we had to find scientists who had the necessary skills to communicate their work. The process required three different steps: scouting for available researchers who fit with the theme of the event; testing their capacity to communicate in a friendly way; and briefing them to ameliorate their natural skills.

Scouting for scientists who carried out studies or made discoveries that fit with the theme of the event was done at a national level – remember that, whatever the level at which your activity is organized (national, local, international etc.), the theme of the event should be respected even if an unrelated amazing discovery could be presented, otherwise you lose the consistency in what you are organizing. We were supported by the CNR's press office, which deals with the writing of public news releases. Many universities, research institutions and research centres have a press office, and you can benefit from their help in the process of scouting for appropriate scientists. The most important element in the decision to take on board a scientist or not is related to the possibility of creating an interactive activity from the studies he or she has carried out.

The testing of the communication skills of scientists was done over the phone. In many cases we used the format of *Famelab* (the science communication competition launched in 2005 at Cheltenham Science Festival), which tests the capacity of scientists to go straight to the point while explaining their scientific advances. The ability to highlight the social impact of their scientific study or discovery was also an important factor we considered, because if scientists are not able to describe why what they do matters to all, it is much harder to capture the attention of ordinary people.

Finally, a briefing session was held prior to the event to train participating scientists to improve their communication skills and in order to make them friendly, able to answer questions easily and open to speak about their hobbies, family and children. We focused on the use of a professional but clear and understandable language to hold the audience's attention. We recommended to scientists that they shift their awareness to the public's perspective, because gaining a listener's point of view of their work makes communication effective.

The stereotype that scientists are a group of nerds isolated from the real world is a strong misconception that could be redressed. Obviously there are scientists who appear to be so, but the majority loves to be involved in communicating their own achievements to the general public and are as passionate about it as any other group of professionals. If popular beliefs about nerdy scientists are debunked, scientific research becomes easier to foster.

2.4 Scientists Do Nothing But Work

Apart from Dr House playing the piano and guitar – and Dr House is not exactly the type of character who can be described as a warm, friendly and welcoming guy! – TV series convey images of scientists as people solely interested in discovering the truth or contributing to the advancement of knowledge.

In general, scientists do not have the reputation of being fun-loving people. The stereotype that they do not have hobbies and friends (apart from their colleagues) is very frequently channelled by TV series and movies. Scientists, by and large, are seen as incapable of having fun, and as being always serious, reflective and removed from everyday commitments. McConnell (2004) has observed that in the eyes of non-scientists science continues to be considered a mind-numbingly boring profession, where work pervades in the scientists' existence, friends fade into the background and hobbies wither.

The stereotype affecting scientists is partially true: during an ongoing experiment or when they are concentrated on finding new solutions, scientists may lose track of time. But these are exceptions to the rule. Scientists tend to be practical, orderly and logical and to be successful through concentration and thoroughness, and not necessarily all the time.

Science requires a high dose of imagination. Creative people are curious, and their curiosity covers a wide range of interests – so much so that many scientists have artistic hobbies. Some are musicians, some draw or paint, some sculpt, some write. The creativity needed in the field of science they are studying or the need to have brilliant ideas to solve scientific problems is also invested in leisure time activities.

Hobbies are essential, according to Runco and Pritzker, because "*a personal correlate for success as a discoverer is hobbies and intensive leisure time activities*" (1999, p.561). In a recent article published in *Nature*, Woolston (2015) emphasizes the benefits of engaging in leisure activities outside of scientific research, because a balance of abilities, as indicated by a range of activities practised at an intensive level, might improve creativity.

When ordinary people interact with scientists during a science communication event, even if scientists are well trained on how to behave, talk and be friendly with the public, the stereotype that researchers are fully immersed in their work remains intact. We should find a way to change this misconception, in order to

Figure 2. Scientists performing at the Globe Science Theatre (All Rights Reserved © IRPPS-Institute for Research on Population and and Social Policies).

dismantle stereotypical images of scientists: what we did was to let people see what scientists do when they do not do science and when they cultivate their hobbies.

At the *Light* event we gave scientists the opportunity to show their talents while performing their hobbies. The words *science* and *fun* are not mutually exclusive, and our event provided ordinary people stimulating encounters with current art and sport practice. Artists and sportspeople performed in a purposively set-up area called the Globe Science Theatre, as shown in Figure 2. Each of the groups of artists and sportspeople on stage had to have at least one member of the performing team actively engaged in scientific research.

The scientists were extremely serious and competent in their performances and the public loved what the scientists were doing.

Following Stebbins (2014)'s definition, most of the scientists were not just hobbyists but were real amateurs, since they were involved in art, sport and entertainment together with professional counterparts. Many of the researchers were distinguished and highly regarded professors, who accepted with enthusiasm to perform in front of the public (for example, at *Light* the President of the Italian National Committee for Sciences and Technologies of Environment and Habitat of CNR danced tango, and one of the authors of this book performed a judo show).

While it is true that researchers from different disciplines spend a lot of time and energy at work – as do many other professionals – they are equally involved in many artistic activities and sports. The passion and energy that scientists put in performing arts or sports helped the public to remove the misconception that scientists are people who have no other interest than their research in their life. Scientists brought to light their human side, showed the public that they do not just live in labs and gave ordinary people the opportunity to understand that every scientific advance is achieved by a group of competent and skilled people who have families, friends and hobbies.

2.5 Breaking The Glass Ceiling

In its Plenary Sitting on 20 July 2015 the European Parliament approved a motion concerning gender imbalances in science (European Parliament 2015). It has been observed that, despite positive changes in recent years, gender equality in science and academia has still not been achieved, with the situation varying across Member States, fields of research and academic grade. In the EU-28, while women account for 59 per cent of university graduates, they account for only 18 per cent of university professors on full professorships. The strikingly low numbers of women in the highest academic and decision-making positions in scientific institutions and universities is also to be noted: this indicates the existence of a glass ceiling, that is an invisible barrier based on prejudices and stereotypes that stands in the way of women accessing positions of responsibility.

To a degree, national laws and the internal rules of the large majority of European research institutions ensure equal treatment for men and women; regulations, however, may control behaviour, but they do not change underlying attitudes. Arguments over the need for gender equality in science continue, and they will not disappear from the academic and political agendas any time soon. The reason for the continued existence of requests for gender equality in science is simple: the fight for equality is not yet won. It is possible for research institutions and organizations to have a facade of gender inclusiveness, yet still perpetuate stereotypes and misconceptions.

Women are under-represented in many fields of science, for example in STEM, and in leadership positions. Changes come about very slowly. In Italy, for example, Palomba calculated that gender parity among academic professors (i.e. 50 per cent of women among professors with full professorships) will be reached in the year 2138, if the current rate of increase in female-held professorships is maintained; 2059 will be the year that gender parity in full professorships is reached in Finland, 2063 the year that it is reached in the UK and 2130 the year that it is reached in Belgium (Palomba 2013).

The European Commission has made considerable efforts to promote a more systematic participation of women in every sector and aspect of scientific activities and research management by ensuring gender balance in decision-making, in order to reach the target of 40 per cent of the under-represented sex in panels and groups and of 50 per cent in advisory groups. In monetary terms, Palomba (2015) calculated that, under the Sixth Framework Programme[1] (FP6), the European Commission invested almost €20 million on projects focused on the promotion of "Women in science"; the amount was increased to €40 million in the Seventh Framework Programme (FP7; Palomba 2015). All these efforts have not yet produced the expected results and women continue to be under-represented in every field of science.

As a consequence, the images of scientists in the minds of non-scientists are persistently masculine. These gender-related stereotypes are reproduced across all ages and across every social group, and ordinary people more often depict scientists as men than as women. The stereotypical images are so embedded in the "cultural brain" that people hold them without being aware of it.

The question is why all these biases persist in the face of an avalanche of evidence that women are good scientists and what can be done to dismantle gender stereotypes in the minds of ordinary people. After all, no one wants to think of themselves as a sexist these days (or at least as sexist enough to be called out for it). Female scientists themselves have difficulty recognizing gender stereotypes in science; there is a certain amount of denial – "It doesn't happen to me" – and female scientists need help recognizing existing gender biases in their department or scientific field.

Over time, in order to describe gender stereotypes in science and their effects on women's careers and achievements, a number of metaphors have been created to represent these gender biases

---

1 Framework Programmes or abbreviated FP1 to FP7 are funding programmes created by the European Commission to support and foster research in the European Research Area. FP6 run for five years from 2002 to 2006; FP7 run for 7 years from 2007 to 2013

and prejudices in the scientific world. The metaphors are the following: the *leaky pipeline*, representing the fact that women disappear from the career track at some point; the *sticky floor*, to describe a discriminatory pattern that keeps women at the bottom of the scientific career ladder; and the *glass ceiling*, the invisible barrier which blocks the advancement of women in science.

Furthermore, there is a constant, unrelenting message sent to women and girls by families, peers, friends and society in general, that is: "You will never be good enough for science. It is too hard for you". After years of hearing this message, it is hard not to internalize it.

We were aware that to address gender stereotypes in science words, numbers or percentages demonstrating how good women are and how much they are penalized while entering or advancing in scientific careers were useless. Plenty of reports, publications, books, articles, public speeches and exhibits on the issue have not significantly changed the situation; the awareness of the gender biases that exist in science has not had obvious effects on academic behaviour.

At the *Light* event, we had to convince ordinary people that women were very good at science, although not being fairly rewarded. We decided to implement two different activities in order to remove existing gender stereotypes about scientists. On one side, mixed-gender teams animated the science corners (in some cases, we had women-only teams), so that women and men were both interacting with the public, thus dismantling the idea that women are not good at science. On the other side, we wanted people to have a direct experience of what it means to be a woman in science, and we thus decided to realize the metaphors on women's careers in science and let people perceive without words the unfairness affecting women who work in scientific labs. All the activities aimed to dislodge the stereotype that science is not for women.

Out of the three main metaphors, we started with the reproduction of the glass ceiling: it was a great success. The term *glass ceiling* comes from the illusion the phenomenon creates: female scientists believe that there are no gender-related obstacles to arrive to top positions while on the contrary there is an invisible barrier (i.e. gender stereotypes) over their heads that prevents them from climbing the institutional hierarchy. The transparency of the glass and the presence of a concrete limit – the ceiling – represent the impossibility for female scientists to reach high-ranking positions; the barrier is not perceived, thus creating an equalitarian appearance and the illusion of an open and meritocratic competition.

Figures 3 and 4 show the metal and glass structure that was designed and realized by Triplan, our partner for the *Light* project. The structure might be considered a work of art. We wanted to represent the following aspects:

- Women in science face career ups and downs; they can see the road to success but perceive it as an uphill struggle.
- Male scientists start at the same level as women, but, at the end of their career, they arrive at higher levels than women. Men face a straight road without obstacles or barriers; they feel they can do it.
- Both men and women see each other, thus creating the illusion that it is possible to cross the wall between them and to change the final result.

The attendees at our event had the opportunity to experience the difference between men's and women's careers in science,

Figure 3. Walking on a career path under a glass ceiling (All Rights Reserved © IRPPS-Institute for Research on Population and and Social Policies).

Figure 4. Final steps of two career paths – one under a glass ceiling (All Rights Reserved © IRPPS-Institute for Research on Population and and Social Policies).

perceiving the difference through their senses. At the end of the experience, they were given explanations. Most of them wanted to repeat the experience from the other gender's perspective (men experiencing the obstacles faced by women; women experiencing the male perspective). It was amazing how much they learned, how many discussions arose among visitors and how easy it was to make them understand the obstacles that female scientists face.

We also planned to realize (though we never did in the end) the other two metaphors: the leaky pipeline and the sticky floor. For the former, it is enough to build two glass tubes, each long enough to create a circuit, and each ending in two transparent containers; one of the tube should have very small holes. The public can pour liquids of two different colours (for example blue and pink, just to follow current gender colour conventions) into the tubes: it goes without saying that the quantity of blue liquid that arrives into the final container from the non-leaky tube will always exceed the quantity of pink liquid that arrives into the other final container, because of the holes in the tube into which the pink liquid is poured. For the metaphor of the sticky floor we thought about creating two ramps of equal height but with different slopes, with women having to climb the steepest slope, which is also made sticky.

Coming back to the stereotype that women are not good enough for science, at the 2010 *Light* event our partner Triplan created an interesting sensorial experience, which was called "Heaven can't wait". It consisted of a 20-metre tunnel made of cloth. It was conceived as an activity aiming to let the wider public understand that gender stereotypes affecting the very nature of science can be removed. The "sensorial tunnel" revolved around the theme of women in science and their careers. The passers-by physically perceived through three senses (touch, hearing and sight) what it means to be a woman in the scientific world. They passed through *Hell*, which represented the gender-related difficulties faced in entering scientific careers, went through the *Purgatory*, which represented the problems occurring once the career has started, and finally they arrived in *Paradise*, where a woman manages to succeed in science. Voices, colours, lights and special floors, ceilings and walls created an immersive space for visitors, facilitating their tour of women's careers in science.

We are convinced that no conference, seminar, workshop or speech made by relevant people can have concrete effects in removing gender stereotypes in science. Male and female scientists themselves easily fall into stereotypical behaviours, which may unintentionally perpetuate women's subordinate status. What we did helps remove misconceptions about gender in science and helps scientists, policy-makers and ordinary people understand both how good women in science are and how many difficulties they face. Although society's message to women that they are inadequate in science is less overt today, a conscious effort is still needed to overcome problems and stereotypes about women. Changing culture takes a long time. If people perceive existing gender unfairness in science and appreciate the work done by women, a significant step forward can be taken.

2.6 Suggestions and Recommendations

Current stereotypes about scientists convey the image that scientists are somehow "different" from ordinary citizens. Scientists are considered socially awkward, isolated and without many friends and interests; science is considered a male profession. The majority of these stereotypes stem from the fact that scientists and non-scientists meet, engage in dialogue and interact very rarely. Our observations and suggestions to undo stereotypes about scientists are the following:

- occasions (i.e. science weeks, science festivals, researchers' nights, science cafés etc.) should be created to favour contacts and interactions between scientists and ordinary people;
- the interactions should be collective experiences that take place between scientists and groups of individuals;
- you should define which stereotypes to undo and the activities you want to implement in order to achieve that goal;
- the venue is extremely important both to attract people and to define your target audience;
- the set-up of the venue acts as a catalyst favouring real interaction between scientists and non-scientists and in producing the expected breaking down of misconceptions about scientists;
- the event must have a theme; the choice of the theme should be made carefully;
- the "why" of the scientific discovery or experiment presented by scientists to the public is as important as the "how";
- scientists who have the natural skills necessary to communicate their work to the wider public must be selected; they must be briefed to ameliorate their natural skills;
- speeches, role models, numbers and exhibits are not enough to eradicate gender stereotypes in science; we

suggest that there should be a number of sensory experiences so that people may have first-hand experience of the gender bias, difficulties and obstacles that women have to face in their scientific career and may form their own opinion.

CHAPTER 3

How to undo young people's stereotypes about scientists and science

Rossella Palomba

3.1 Making Science "Cool"

Stereotypes about scientists are not completely negative and under certain circumstances they may well be considered positive: who does not like to be smart, able to solve crimes with formulas and equations, as in the TV series *Numbers*, or famous for discoveries that have solved the biggest problems of humankind? The issue is that these stereotypes imply positive qualities that are so extremely positive that they set the bar unrealistically high and can inhibit young people's aspirations to be part of the group. "I am not a genius, I cannot be a researcher", "I am not clever

---

How to cite this book chapter:
Palomba, R 2017 How to undo young people's stereotypes about scientists and science. In: Tintori, A and Palomba, R. *Turn on the light on science*, Pp. 51–63. London: Ubiquity Press. DOI: https://doi.org/10.5334/bba.d. License: CC-BY 4.0

enough to be good at science" or "Science is too difficult for a girl like me" are some of the phrases that exemplify how extremely positive qualities can leave ordinary people feeling apart.

Inaccurate stereotypes exist around the STEM sector and its role in society: on the one hand STEM is not perceived, by both boys and girls, as a field where there is passion for discovery, but rather as a dry, fact-based matter ; on the other hand, girls are not encouraged to the same extent as boys to embark on a scientific career, in particular in STEM.

The widely held view that scientists are smart, combined with the commonly held stereotype that they are exceptional individuals, may prevent many young people from considering careers in science as a life opportunity. The popular idea that science careers are only for the very clever few is strengthened by the limited awareness young people have of the broad range of possibilities (both in and beyond science) that scientific careers can lead to. Families also lack the necessary information to encourage their children towards science and technology. In a study on young people's science aspirations, ASPIRES (2013, p.30) concluded that *"children from families possessing medium or high science capital are more likely to aspire to science and STEM related careers"*. Conversely, because the majority of children do not come from families with medium or high science capital, they are not expected to show any interest or to be excited about science, innovation and technology as a future career opportunity – and yet Great Britain is one of the best places in the world to do science.

Since 2001 the European Commission has highlighted the lack of interest of young Europeans in science and technology related careers (European Commission 2001). In the Eurobarometer survey on young people's aspirations (see European Commission 2007a), unattractive and difficult science education in schools was identified as the main reason for this. Since then, across Europe, many actions have been taken. According to Valente (2015), under the Sixth Framework Programme almost €20 million have been spent on a number of initiatives aimed at increasing the proportion of students in the STEM sector. Under the Seventh Framework Programme the amount of money spent by the European Commission on this aim increased, to more than €90 million. The initiatives included measures aimed at increasing students' interest in STEM at school, engaging students in activities that raised awareness of STEM jobs and organizing STEM fairs or European science weeks for families and children (Valente 2015).

Despite the European Commission's efforts, the results are not yet satisfactory. As observed by Deloitte (2014), in 2012, while a steady and considerable growth in the share of 30- to 34-year-olds who have successfully completed university or other tertiary-level education took place in the EU, only 23 per cent of all EU-28 graduates held STEM qualifications (a slight increase from 22 per cent in 2007). Cultural stereotypes that deter young people from being fascinated by science and becoming scientists seem hard to remove.

The European Commission gave special attention to the aim of attracting girls into scientific research, and into STEM in particular. According to Eurostat (2015), within the EU-28 close to three fifths of all graduates in 2015 were women, while male graduates accounted for three fifths of the total number of graduates for the science, mathematics and computing fields, and close to three quarters of the total for engineering, manufacturing and construction-related fields. In the EU-27 women remain largely under-represented (at 32 per cent of the workforce) in scientific research and innovation (Eurostat 2015).

Women and girls shun science, technology, engineering, and mathematics, and their presence is low at all levels of the STEM career pipeline, from the interest to study a STEM discipline to having a career in a STEM field once adult. As observed by Correll (2004), cultural stereotypes and the attitudes of women themselves make the challenge of having more female scientists tougher. There are many societal beliefs about how women do not have strong mathematical ability and about how men make better engineers and scientists (Correll 2004). Girls are not encouraged by families to embark on a science career, because such a career is considered too hard for girls; peers look down on them as weird for taking that interest.

The OECD has noted that young people generally have a positive view of science and technology, but that the image of STEM as a profession is largely negative (OECD 2008). Positive contacts with science and technology at an early age can have a long-lasting impact, while negative experiences at school, due to uninteresting content or poor teaching, are often very detrimental to future choices.

In the last decade, given the challenge of increasing the number of young people entering scientific careers, numerous initiatives at the national and European levels have been taken to inspire young people about science and make careers in science and technology attractive for them. The initiatives varied both in content and in aims: some were focused on the challenges facing education systems and the need to modernize pedagogical methods; others on enhancing the professional profile of teachers. A number of initiatives were launched to promote partnerships between schools, universities and industry and projects to improve female participation in STEM courses and careers. This series of activities is still yielding weak results and is not aimed at undoing the stereotypes affecting the image of scientists and the content of science.

In order to undo stereotypes that prevent young people from embarking on scientific careers, special attention should be given to two sets of initiatives carried out at the EU level: the awards to young students aiming to give visibility to the creativity and imagination of younger generations, and the organization of fairs aiming to arouse interest in science within younger age groups and to encourage them to embark on research careers.

Since 1989 the European Commission has organized a contest called the European Union Contest for Young Scientists (EUCYS) with the goal of promoting cooperation and exchange among young scientists and guiding them towards a future career in science and technology. Every year, approximately 200 students attending European high schools enter the competition in the hope of winning awards. The awards are of monetary kind: in 2015 the awards were €7,000 for the first-prize winning teams, and €5,000 and €3,500 for the second- and third-placed teams respectively.

Awards are also given at the national level, including at The Big Bang Fair in the UK, "I giovani e le scienze" ("Youth and Science") in Italy, "Unge Forskere" ("Young Scientists") in Denmark and "Jugend forscht" ("Youth research") in Germany. In such events, small teams of students (usually at secondary level) are invited to research and develop STEM projects of their own choice over several months, and then to display the results of their work at a dedicated fair.

The preparation of the projects is often done through after-school science clubs or in the students' personal time. As observed by Joyce and Dzoga (2011), the projects are chiefly tackled outside school, so those students with home environments that encourage STEM (e.g. if parents are working in scientific careers or have interests in science) can be disproportionally advantaged compared to students whose family awareness of STEM is not as conducive to understanding the value of engaging with extracurricular activities. In some cases, the projects remain at the planning stage, without the production of a functioning prototype.

Though improvements can be made to better integrate such initiatives into normal class activities, there is no doubt that the existence of student competitions helps generate interest in the sciences and increases the understanding of the relevance of science to real-world issues among all students. Last but not least, it facilitates the overcoming of stereotypes concerning science careers and encourages young people to embark on research-related studies and careers.

Alongside the contests, many science fairs where small teams of students, usually at secondary level, also research and develop STEM projects of their own choice take place around Europe. The fairs are linked to national or local student contests and EUCYS then links to national science fairs, thus creating a pyramid of merit and talent among European young people. The fairs target both students in school with their teachers and parents who visit the fair with their children. They are an opportunity for bright students to showcase their abilities, creativity and imagination and might be a motivational tool to engage those students who are lagging behind in STEM disciplines.

3.2 Inv-Factor: A Contest For Young Inventors

Who does not know *The X Factor*, the television music competition whose title refers to the indefinable "something" that makes for star quality? Millions of European boys and girls like the competition and watch TV to follow other boys and girls dancing, singing and explaining that they have a dream: to become a star in the field of music. The message one can draw from that TV show is "If you really want to be a singer or a TV star, you can do it". Obviously reality is different, and a lot of talent is needed, together with a lot of work that has to be put into nurturing that talent. Nevertheless, the TV programme is brilliantly made; it is addictive and compelling.

We thought that something similar might be done in the field of science with the aim of dismantling the stereotypes concerning scientists and science careers. The messages would have to be "If you really want to be a scientist, you can do it" and "Science is the most fantastic work you can do". Within the framework of the *Light* project, we organized a contest to look for the special "something" that makes for scientist material. The contest was called INV-Factor, because we were looking for the capacity to be an inventor and gave out awards for inventiveness and imagination.

In our opinion two aspects of existing contests and student fairs should be improved: the awards should not be monetary, and only school or classroom teams should be eligible for the contest. Regarding the first aspect, it should be noted that the main reward for scientists – as for creative people in general – is emotion, not financial incentives: it is the feeling of making progress every day towards a meaningful goal. As shown by Pink (2009), studies carried out over 40 years back up the idea that, for most tasks, you cannot incentivize people to perform better, create and innovate with money – this is one of the most robust findings from social science, but also the most ignored.

Regarding the second point, we know that one of the best parts of the job of scientists is getting to work with other scientists and sharing ideas with other people. The best ideas no longer come from solitary researchers, and it is clear that all of us together are smarter than each one of us individually. In spite of this reality, when boys or girls think about scientists, the picture that pops into their heads is that of a solitary scientist, an isolated genius, working on some world-changing solution to a problem. For centuries, the Western model of science has been simple: we relied on geniuses; our most revolutionary breakthroughs have typically emerged from individuals, working by themselves. This is not true anymore, but the false picture has remained in people's minds, becoming a deep-rooted stereotype.

In order to undo the stereotypes concerning scientists held by young people, we have to change this picture and let them experience that being a scientist means being part of a team, working together to figure out something new. Young students do teamwork at school, and we thus decided to create a contest for schools. Teams who intended to participate in our competition had to present the products of the work they had done with their classmates and teachers during school time.

As monetary rewards are not appropriate to encourage young students to embark on scientific careers, we thought that the best award for the winners of INV-Factor was to let the young inventors participate in a great science communication event together with adult scientists.

The segregation of young people's creativity in purposively organized fairs puts young participants on a secondary level in respect to adult researchers and conveys the following message: "You are too young to invent something really interesting". There are many examples demonstrating how wrong this stereotypical idea is. Think of Mark Zuckerberg, the creator of Facebook, or just look around on the internet: you will be amazed by the number of teens who spent their time and energy to create new things to make a better world for everyone. There is no doubt that, when it comes to inventing, it is not age, but being a visionary, that counts – and this is exactly the quality we were looking for with the INV-Factor contest.

The contest was organized in three steps. We started by announcing it on a dedicated website and on the CNR website. The contest's rules were published online; the media were informed by press releases from the CNR and the Representation of the European Commission in Italy.

The rules of the contest specify the following details and requirements:

- the contest aims at stimulating and enhancing the scientific creativity of 15- to 19-year-old students;
- we want functioning prototypes of inventions, and not just brilliant ideas;
- the students should have acquired at school the scientific knowledge and competencies needed to conceive and realize the inventions;
- the contest is primarily aimed at vocational and technological high schools, though all high schools are eligible;
- classroom or school teams are eligible for the contest; isolated inventors are not excluded, but they should be supported and mentored by a teacher from their school (to be honest, we never had proposals coming from individual geniuses!);
- in the application for the contest a representative of the classroom team should be identified to facilitate contacts between the organizers and the students;
- inventorship and ownership of the invention go to all team members.

When the teams applied to participate in INV-Factor they had to very briefly describe their idea and how they intended to realize it, the school where they studied and the team composition. A committee of noted researchers, mainly – though not exclusively – from the CNR, made a first selection. Candidates could be asked directly to give additional information in order to better illustrate their idea. The teams that were considered eligible for INV-Factor were then asked to realize a functioning prototype of their invention, to be presented at the final contest.

Four months later, the second step was launched and the selected teams were asked to send home videos, photos and drawings of the prototypes of their inventions, as well as presentation slides and a text of maximum 1,000 characters describing their work. On the basis of the material presented, the panel of five INV-Factor judges, which consisted of three CNR research directors, one representative of the Representation of the European Commission in Italy and one representative of the small and medium-sized enterprises' association, selected ten inventions.

The final step was the core of the contest. We organized something similar to the *X Factor* live performances of competitors in front of judges and other contestants. We are convinced that every team should be aware of what the other teams did and of why the panel of judges arrived to the final decision, awarding one team instead of the others.

All the inventions were exhibited on the premises of the Representation of the European Commission in Italy in Rome. The panel of judges went from one invention to the other, asked questions, checked the functioning of the prototypes and asked for technical information. The media were also invited and a large number of journalists from newspapers, TV channels and radio stations, both local and national, were present.

The panel of experts evaluated the inventions on the basis of three criteria listed in the regulations: novelty from a technological point of view; feasibility of the invention; and social impact of the invention. The preparation and competency of the teams was also tested. In a conference room, each team had exactly five minutes to give a slideshow presentation about their invention in front of judges, the media and other competitors. The idea is that if you know what you have done and why, you should be able to describe it in five minutes and convince the judges that your invention is the best. A well balanced mixture of communication skills, competency and determination was thus evaluated.

It is to be noted that special attention was given to the sex composition of the teams and a special award was given to female inventors. Women are generally less competitive than men, and this could affect their desire to participate in a competition where boys are the majority (in Italian vocational schools, boys are the majority). We encouraged female participation, ensured gender equal opportunities in winning the award and dedicated a special prize to girls.

Regarding the inventions, we were amazed by the fact that the teens were so attentive to recent news, facts and stories. For example, a student team invented a device to save lives, after learning how many babies die from heat-related deaths after being trapped inside vehicles because the drivers forgot the children were there; another team invented an alcohol-measuring device combined with an ignition interlock that prevents vehicles from starting if the driver has alcohol on his or her breath. Young people were also willing to solve problems for people with disabilities: a team invented a device that can guide blind people, only requiring them to wear a simple special hat; another team created a special wheelchair that can be guided by voice. Mobile phones are another attractive topic; among others, let us mention an invention to charge mobile phones through the energy generated by walking, the inventors of which – all girls – were knighted by the President of the Italian Republic.

As mentioned above, the award for the winners of the contest was to participate in *Light*. The boys and girls were thrilled by the opportunity to be side by side with adult scientists, and many of them expressed the intention to choose a scientific faculty for further study and the desire to follow a scientific career. Exploring career options is an important step on the road to adulthood. Science is considered to be difficult, and the general opinion is that you need to have talent for science (a special gift), otherwise you will not be successful. We do hope that INV-Factor has contributed to change this image.

3.3 Suggestions and Recommendations

Scientists are imagined by young students as isolated geniuses or people who must have special talents to do their job. In the minds of teens, science allows little space for factors such as intuition, imagination and creativity and deals more with hard facts. At the time of career choice this stereotyped view of science and scientists could have an important influence on discouraging young people (and girls in particular) from embarking on scientific careers. The European Commission has launched various initiatives to attract young Europeans towards the sciences and science careers. Among other initiatives, we think that contests concerning inventions made by teens are valuable tools for overcoming the "science is too difficult for me" stereotype. The following are our suggestions to undo young people's stereotypes about scientists:

- one of the best tools to break down the stereotype that science is for the very clever and talented few is to showcase the creativity and inventiveness of the teens;
- contests aimed at stimulating and enhancing the scientific creativity of 15- to 19-year-old students are a great opportunity to show the potential of younger generations and to overcome the "I am not a genius, I cannot be a scientist" stereotype;
- girls should be encouraged to participate in the contest and equal opportunities should be ensured;
- the importance of the collaborative nature of scientific and technological work should be stressed and the contests should be addressed to classroom or school teams;
- awards of monetary nature should be avoided;
- the segregation of young inventors in dedicated fairs is in conflict with the idea that creativity is not related to age.

CHAPTER 4

Can people really change their opinion about scientists?

Antonio Tintori

Large public outreach events such as the ones we organized are exciting ways to engage the public in interacting with scientists. These events are relatively easy to promote and share with a broad audience using internet tools and social media, as well as using "traditional" communication tools (i.e. advertisements on newspapers, radio spots, street posters etc.).

The general public seems increasingly interested in knowing about science, what it means and what are the consequences of recent scientific discoveries on their everyday life. But, while science holds an esteemed place among citizens and policy-makers,

How to cite this book chapter:
Tintori, A 2017 Can people really change their opinion about scientists?. In: Tintori, A and Palomba, R. *Turn on the light on science*, Pp. 65–88. London: Ubiquity Press. DOI: https://doi.org/10.5334/bba.e. License: CC-BY 4.0

the stereotypes affecting the image of scientists persist. Although the skills and work of scientists are highly respected, that admiration does not seem to extend to other aspects of their lives. As we have seen in the previous chapters, the charming and charismatic scientist is not a common image in popular culture, and the entertainment industry often portrays scientists as unattractive, reclusive and socially inept individuals.

Image has a lot to do with how effective communication is in capturing the attention of the public. The more appealing the image, the more likely that people will listen to what is being said and shown. This is why the European Commission funds activities like the ones we implemented through specific programmes of action.

But did the implemented activities really help in changing the image of scientists to a more positive one? In order to answer this question we have to carry out an evaluation. Several reports from recent large outreach events (see for example Sardo and Grand 2014; Castell et al. 2014; Koolstra 2008) show that science communication events lead policy-makers, institutions and the general public to want to know more about what participants are gaining from these activities and about the overall impact of these efforts.

Therefore, there is an increasing interest in gaining insight in how science communication events attended by the public can be evaluated. In many cases, for example when the European Commission promotes and funds projects and events, the evaluation of the effects of the activities is mandatory. In addition, the evaluation may help event organizers to gain new ideas on how to adjust specific elements of the events, to make them more effective in the future.

Evaluation is the measurement of how relevant the implemented actions were in causing change. It serves the dual function of providing a basis for improving the quality of future activities, and a tool to verify achievements against intended results. The more accurate and reliable the gathered information is, the more the evaluation will help to build a solid basis for improvement.

In our case, the informal nature of the event, the various types of activities and the little possibility of control over their implementation (implementation which relies on the capacities and creativity of the researchers) make traditional evaluation (i.e. posing questions to rate visitors' satisfaction and ask general information about event logistics) far from ideal to understand the true impact of these events. Measuring the complete impact of initiatives that involve multiple and different activities, all of which operate in mutually reinforcing ways, is more complex than taking a snapshot of a given activity's effectiveness. Only the whole initiative's different parts and the ways they interact may tell the whole story. Moreover, we aimed to change and measure a highly complex issue, that of stereotypes about scientists – a difficult task.

Nevertheless, a high-quality evaluation of impact that is made by professionals and carefully conducted and analysed may provide a basis to understand which aspects of science communication initiatives have worked (in our case in breaking down stereotypes about scientists and science), and for which audience.

4.1 Goals and Design of the Evaluation Study

Defining the goals and objectives of any event is essential in deciding how to measure its impact. If the event is part of a more general programme, its goals should be aligned with the ones of the general programme. Under the Marie Skłodowska-Curie Actions programme, the European Commission funds and supports the European Researchers' Night, whose aim is to bring together the general public and the exciting world of research and innovation and to show that science is fun and accessible to everyone. The activities must increase awareness of research and innovation, with a view to support the public recognition of researchers, create an understanding of the impact of researchers' work on daily life and encourage young people to embark on scientific careers.

Though not explicitly mentioned, the suppression or reduction of stereotypes about scientists in the minds of members of the general public is a necessary action to take to make the interaction between scientists and the general public effective. Therefore, our aim to dislodge stereotypical images of scientists was well aligned to the European Commission's general objectives, and our project was funded.

Evaluation studies may pertain to various types of possible effects deriving from being exposed to specific activities. Many effects may be evaluated by an impact analysis technique, such as changes in knowledge, attitudes and/or behaviour. Our evaluation study was aimed at determining whether the following main goals were achieved: a) would visiting the event lead to a more positive image of science and scientists among attendees?; and b) how would the visitors experience and judge the event? Therefore, we focused our interest on the effects pertaining to the public image of science and scientists.

The evaluation assessment took place through interviews with visitors of the event; outside experts were entrusted with this task to ensure the impartiality of the results. The feedback was collected using semi-structured evaluation questionnaires consisting of 14 questions and delivered face-to-face by professional interviewers. Visitors were interviewed about their experiences at the event and about their attitudes regarding the public image of science and scientists. The impact analysis activities involved the following three steps:

1) defining the questionnaire;
2) conducting the interviews;
3) analysing the results.

The interviews were held when attendees were leaving the location of the event, i.e. immediately after the event; this gave us the possibility to perform the evaluation in a more personal and qualitative manner.

The sections of the questionnaire were the following:

a) socio-demographic profile of the visitors;
b) event assessment;
c) through which information channels used in the promotion of the event had the respondents learned about the event;
d) perception of respondents about stereotypes that pertain to the life and work of researchers;
e) reflections and suggestions for future initiatives.

Our "operational approach" in designing the impact assessment activities responded to two specific needs:

- the usability of the instrument: as the questionnaire was intended as a research instrument able to investigate the perceptions and the comments of very different respondents, its usability implied simplicity in its structure and in the language and rapidity in the submission and collection of answers;
- the wide range of topics to be treated: in order to provide a picture of attendees' perceptions on science and

scientists and their recommendations for the improvement of future and similar events, the questionnaire was designed to contain sections on the profiles of respondents, their perceptions and comments and suggestions for future improvement.

Usability and complexity are not easy to integrate; our questionnaire was an attempt to respond to these two antithetic objectives. The integration of these objectives has resulted in a questionnaire which has proved to be easy to submit, quick to compile and rich in information. The questionnaire was a semi-structured one, to allow participants to give responses in their own words. It was designed in such a way that participants had freedom to express their views when answering the questions, without any influence or clues from the interviewers. Some questions were open-ended to allow the respondents to give either positive or negative answers. The interviews were carried out by experienced researchers, trained on the specific objectives of the survey, who could carry out a qualitative interview.

A key characteristic of every science communication event is their fleeting nature and at the same time the temporal "validity" of the change in attitudes (i.e. if it is permanent or not). Lasting effects of the event cannot be measured with our approach, but the methodology that guided our interviews provided the possibility of getting a good idea of how visitors perceived the event and its messages.

The survey included questions about whether respondents had been exposed to all or part of the activities, as well as questions on the public reputation of scientists in general, on the researchers' work, on the effectiveness of the event and also about the attendees' personal considerations inspired by our activities.

Additionally, participants' motivations for attending the event were also considered.

Asking about background characteristics such as age, sex and educational level provided us the possibility to determine whether visitors of the event could be compared with their peers in general and whether possible effects would differ between subgroups defined on the basis of these background characteristics. We measured whether the experience had produced more effects on male or female visitors, and on younger or older ones, and we crossed the data with other variables such as education level.

As mentioned before, the survey was conducted at the moment when attendees left the location of the event. Using this method allowed us to receive feedback from a large number of participants. However, there were unavoidable problems of sampling bias, because only those who were willing to be interviewed and had time for it were included in the survey – for example, it was very difficult to gather feedback from people leaving the event late in the night. An electronic evaluation questionnaire delivered by means of a Computer-Assisted Web Interviewing (CAWI) system that attendees may fill out once at home may overcome this problem, but the validity of such an electronic evaluation is under question.

A total of 1,087 face-to-face interviews were conducted for *Light' 13*. The event's assessment was therefore conducted on over 5 per cent of the audience (the 2013 edition of the event hosted about 20,000 visitors). Over 95 per cent of respondents filled up the full questionnaire; this high percentage is probably due to the survey's short length and the willingness of respondents to express their feelings about the experience they just had. The respondents profile plays a fundamental role in the impact assessment, as it provides – when crossed with other data – precious information on the attitudes and expectations of specific groups of visitors in relation to the various implemented activities. The profiles revealed that 58 per cent of the respondents were female and 42 per cent were male; the majority of people interviewed were in the 21- to 30-years-old age group (25 per cent), which was followed by the less than 20-years-old age group (22 per cent of respondents).

The event started at 5.00 p.m. The first interview was completed at 6.18 p.m., when the first visitor left the location. It has been estimated that the average duration of a visit was 2h30 with a maximum visit duration of 4h49 among housewives and almost 3h among the more highly educated visitors.

4.2 Can People Change their Attitudes Towards Scientists?

An important section of the questionnaire was designed to acquire a clear understanding of the respondents' perceptions and points of view on a crucial issue: the image of science and scientists within the civil society. The importance of science and scientific knowledge is gradually increasing, and by consequence the importance of the scientists who give a direction to science and scientific activities is also increasing. Stakeholders, policy-makers, and researchers themselves strive for the general public to have positive images of scientists.

We know from the last Eurobarometer survey on science and technology that more than one fourth of Europeans consider scientists to be too focused on extremely complicated and specific scientific issues: scientists are seen as remote from society, unable to look at problems from a wider perspective and responsible for locking themselves up in ivory towers of knowledge; in addition, more than half of Europeans think that scientific knowledge gives scientists an extremely dangerous power (Eurobarometer 2010). Therefore, the image of scientists is far from positive and stereotypes are present and strong. On the contrary, science has an indisputable high reputation among Europeans and the majority of respondents in the Eurobarometer survey are convinced that science and innovation can sort out every problem and make our lives better (Eurobarometer 2010). There is an evident gap between the image of science and that of scientists, who are the ones who make science possible. The main goal is therefore to stimulate people's minds to portray a new public image of scientists, closing the gaps between scientific research and the civil society.

We implemented the activities described in the previous chapters in order to improve the image of scientists, to make people change attitudes towards scientists and to make scientists feel closer and friendly. We will present the results of the 2013 event here. Since we started the experience in 2008, we also give comparisons with the previous years' surveys when appropriate.

Despite the fundamental role played by science in society, an extremely high percentage of interviewees (77 per cent) declared that scientists are shown scarcely any appreciation in our society. Respondents with a higher level of education are more aware of the lack of public recognition of scientists; they are without doubt better informed about technological and scientific developments and more sensitive to the need to improve the perception of the role of scientists in society at large.

Since 2008, our event has attracted an audience with a very high level of education: 76 per cent of the respondents have at least a university degree or a postgraduate one beyond a master's degree. It is to be noted that Italy is a country where a small percentage of the population holds a university degree: the fact that the event attracted mainly graduates is a point of weakness of our action. A better-planned communication campaign, tailored to a wider audience, might have increased the participation of less educated people. However, because visitors to our events were a self-selected part of the general population, their attitudes may well be considered as being the most advanced ones. This aspect reinforces the conclusion that the widespread perception of the lack of public attention to scientists' societal role needs specific interventions from institutions and policy-makers. Public opinion is often only mobilized when research and new discoveries raise ethical questions; on the contrary, the public needs to be properly informed on the general work of scientists, so that it can make up its mind about the relevance of science and scientists, break down stereotypes and open up new lines of communication with the scientific community.

Our activities increased the general public's knowledge and understanding of the benefits of scientific research and the work of scientists. Around 80 per cent of respondents declared that their participation in the event contributed to them having a clearer view of what the work of researchers consists of. All our efforts to make the interaction between scientists and the general public easier and effective were thus rewarded. Scientists were able to overcome their institutional reticence and let their voices be heard beyond the restricted forum of scholars and colleagues.

As observed by the science communicator Feliú-Mójer (2015), when scientists are able to communicate effectively beyond their peer groups to broader, non-scientist audiences, it builds support for science, promotes understanding of its wider relevance to society and encourages more informed decision-making at all levels, from government to communities to individuals. What we achieved is well in line with the more general goals of the European Commission related to the need to create a bridge between civil society and the scientific research community. We offered scientists the possibility to improve their interactions with the public: we trained them on how to better communicate and we created an easy channel for interaction, and they were able to manage well.

The crucial question to answer is: did we really change people's minds towards researchers? Half of the respondents declared that the event has contributed to change image they had of researchers in a positive manner. The positive change concerning the image of scientists is remarkable among teens and less evident among the 20- to 40-year-old age group, as shown in Graph 1; the former result is an important achievement and the latter calls for new actions aimed at changing the attitudes towards scientists of those aged between 20 and 40.

When we compare the 2013 results with the ones collected in the previous years, we find that what we have done has contributed in a remarkable way to change the image of scientists for an extremely relevant and increasing number of visitors. A statistical analysis of the historical trend of answers to this question allows us to check for changes in the stereotypical views of scientists held by laypeople. A six-year period was analysed: from 2008 to 2013. In this period the percentage of visitors who declare that our activity is a helpful and necessary tool in changing the public image of science and scientists grows steadily, as shown in Graph 2.

In recent years, attention towards scientific progress has increased, and this fact may have positively affected our data. However, in the same period we observed a clear persistence of stereotypes about science both from statistical data coming from national and European surveys and during meetings that we

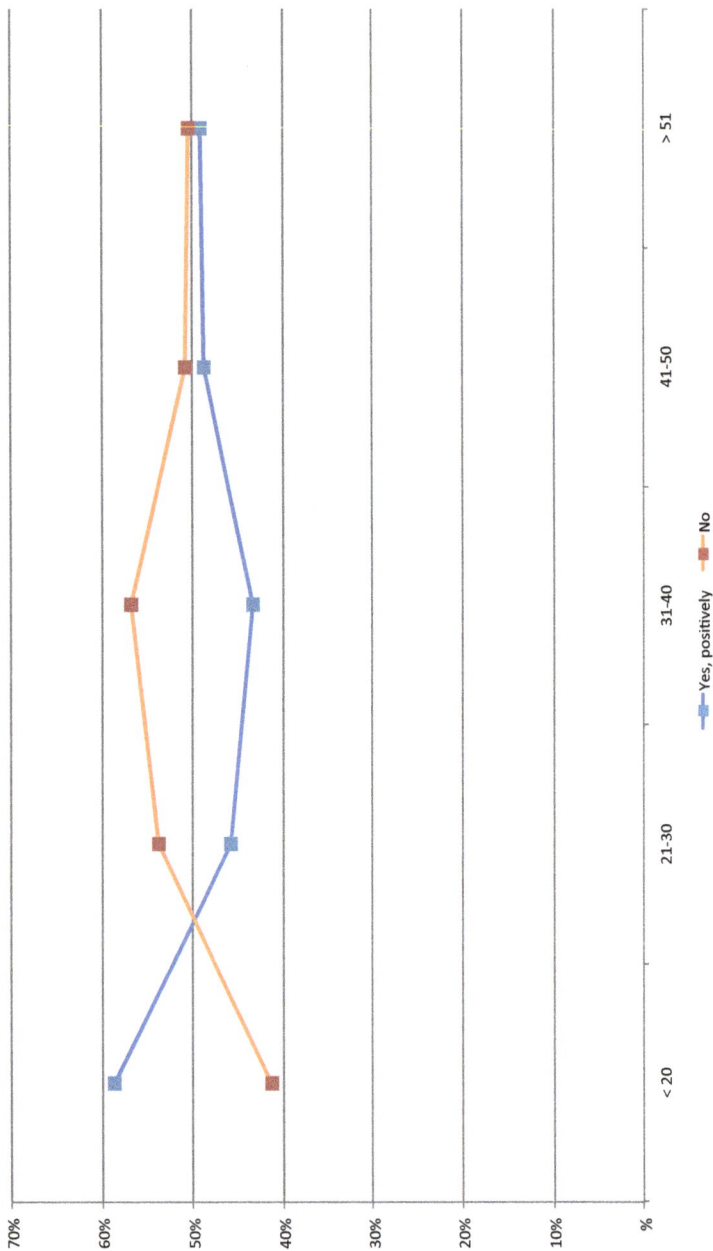

Graph 1. Does the event help to change the image of researchers? (percentages of responses by age).

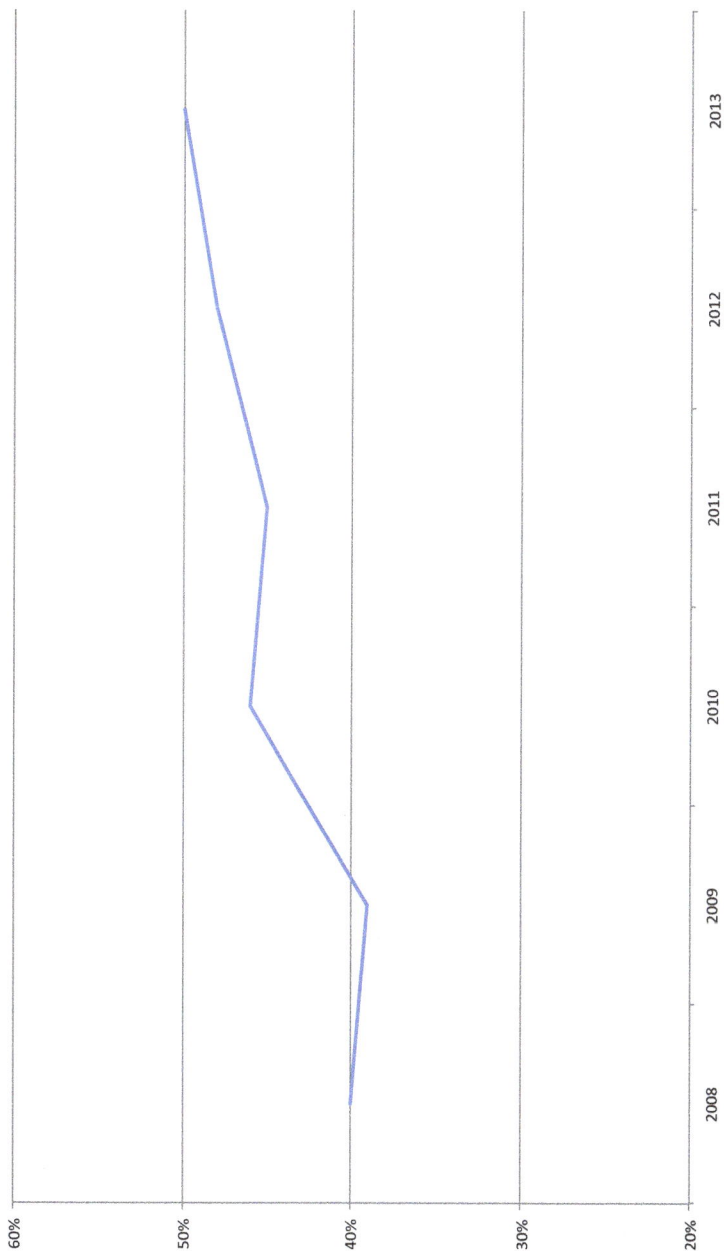

Graph 2. Does the event help to change the image of researchers positively? (percentage of "Yes, positively" answers, 2008–2013).

organized with students for the promotion of scientific careers (particularly STEM ones). This is why our activism in dismantling stereotypical images of scientists seems very timely, and hopefully efficient in producing change. Year after year, our research team was involved in breaking down stereotypes about scientists and science and improving the effectiveness of the actions aimed at achieving this goal. The trend illustrated in Graph 2 shows a positive step in this direction.

The growing number of visitors, all curious and enthusiastic about scientific discoveries, also testifies to the success of our initiative. We created the right atmosphere to facilitate the interaction between scientists and citizens, combining scientific complexity with entertainment. The impact of scientists' work on the everyday life of citizens was also highlighted.

One third of our respondents had already participated in the previous years' events from 2009 onwards: this shows a "loyalty" behaviour in this type of activities. In order to undo stereotypes about scientists, it is very important to not only attract first-time visitors, but also retain previous attendees over the years. In fact, people who have been repeatedly exposed to the event's messages said they had changed their ideas regarding science and the work of researchers significantly and positively (9 out of 10 of the respondents who visited the previous years' events reported this change). Again, this is an interesting result that demonstrates that it is possible to achieve a positive change in attitudes towards scientists.

It is very important to "set" the attitudinal change by repeatingly exposing the lay audience to activities aimed at breaking down the stereotypical image of scientists. While there is a clear reduction of stereotypes related to scientists among those who participated many times in our activities, the event's visit duration is another variable that influences the effectiveness of the exposure. As already mentioned, it has been estimated that the average duration of the event visit was of 2h30'. From the survey, it emerged that the percentage of people who considered the event able to change the image of scientists was higher in the group who visited the event for more than the average time than in the group whose visit length was below the average (64 per cent of respondents in the former group, compared to 50 per cent in the latter).

In our events, we combined scientific experiments and demonstrations with entertainment. Scientists entertained the public by dancing, playing music and performing sports and arts. They showed they had hobbies that offered them a vital escape from the laborious life of their labs, and that they take their hobbies very seriously. It has been observed that the average scientist is not statistically more likely than a member of the general public to have an artistic or sport hobby, but that the more accomplished a scientist is, the more likely he or she is to have one. Root-Bernstein (2008) has calculated that Nobel Prize winning scientists are 2.85 times more likely than the average scientist to have an artistic or crafty hobby. A recent paper by Scheffer et al. (2015) suggests that artistic engagement develops talents that are necessary to be a more creative scientist.

It is very important to let scientists show their human and friendly face in order to change the image of scientists positively in non-scientists' minds. Generally, contacts between non-scientists and researchers take place in laboratories: citizens go to meet scientists in labs during special events or science festivals. Although visiting a research centre can be an enriching experience, this approach is cold and puts the audience in a listening position. It is very different to see a well known physicist or biologist dancing, acting or playing musical instruments: it facilitates a more open interaction and engagement between science, scientists and the general public. The best quality of any scientist is their "humanity" applied in solving problems and achieving new results for the benefit of everyone. The communication of this humanity is what we were striving for.

As expected, visitors to our event appreciated in particular the scientific experiments area (61 per cent), while only 35 per cent preferred the scientists' artistic and sport performances. This result is encouraging and goes exactly in the direction we wanted. It shows that the public is not motivated to come to our event purely for entertainment, but because it is an occasion where science and citizens meet, a place where the public and the researchers interact and have fun, a place where the experience is mainly about bilateral communication. This encounter between seemingly distant worlds generates a stimulating relationship and is full of new meanings for the visitors, who learn a new way to be and to do science.

Attending entertainment shows and scientists' artistic and sports performances at the Globe Science Theatre – a relevant part of our format for breaking down the stereotypes about scientists – has proved to be an influential variable for changing the image of researchers. Although the public expressed a clear preference for the experimental-science area compared to the performances' area, the stereotypes have been most questioned in the minds of attendees who went to both areas: interaction with researchers showing both the public and the private spheres of their lives helped to spread a new and more realistic idea of scientific work and of who scientists are in about 7 out of 10 visitors. Coming to and participating in our activities more than once, visiting the event for more than two hours (the average time) and taking part in different experiences are all elements that have proved to be useful in changing the image of researchers positively.

Respondents were very positive towards the proposed format of the event. About 8 out of 10 respondents said they felt it was very appropriate to combine the figure of the researcher with an entertainment event; 40 per cent were even excited about this unusual format, as shown in Graph 3.

It is common sense that there is no simple relationship between knowledge of science and the acceptance or appreciation of science and scientists. Today's approaches in science communication are dialogue-oriented and focused on interaction, which is considered the greatest predictor of positive learning outcomes for attendees. We are convinced that what we did represented a successful mediating point to start a profitable dialogue between citizens and scientists and to create a more positive image of researchers and their work.

4.3 Assessing The Impact on Young People

In general, students love science, they study science at school, watch sci-fi and are usually attracted by discoveries. Young people choose scientific university courses, but few of them plan to pursue a scientific career. This is of course a very urgent issue, because the more science we do, the more scientists we will need. The lack of interest in scientific careers among young people is due to different reasons, but there is mainly a lack of awareness about the work of scientists. Our event was considered fundamental in convincing young people to embark on a scientific

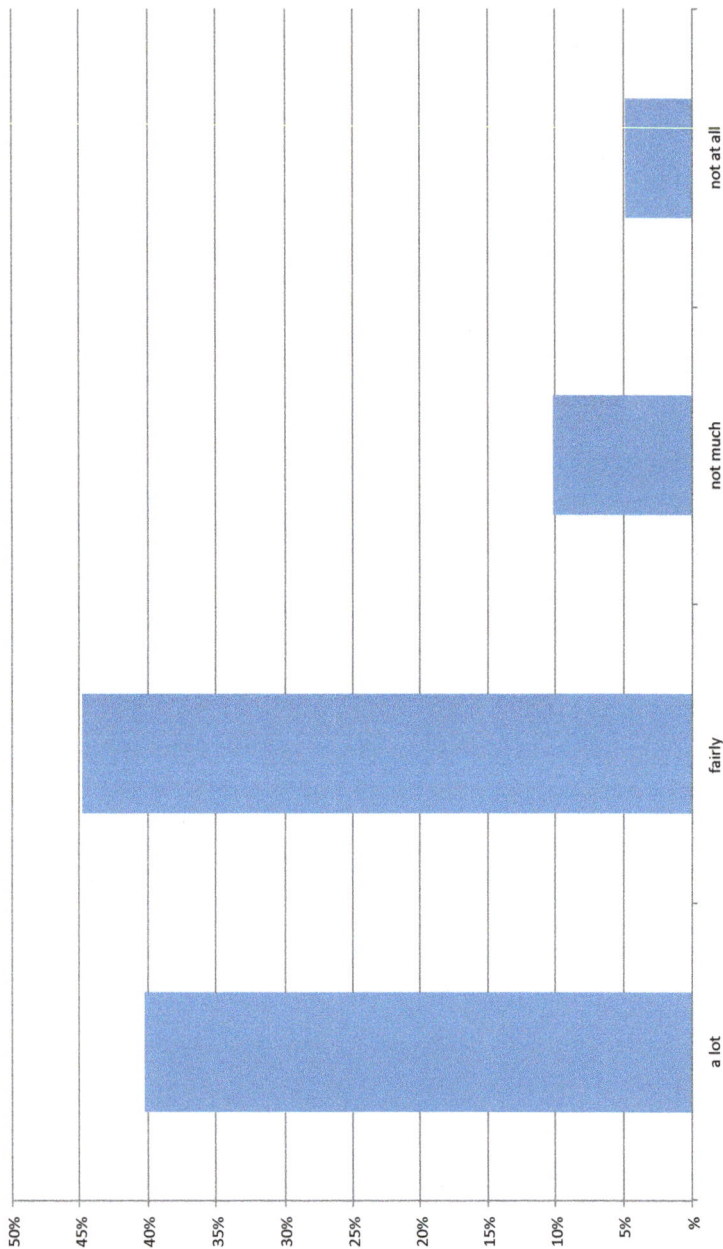

Graph 3. Is it appropriate to combine the image of scientists with an entertainment event? (answers in percentages).

career by 43 per cent of respondents (and fairly important in doing so by 41 per cent).

Looking at the impact of the event on the less than 20-years-old age group, we note that a large majority of young respondents (78 per cent) stated that they changed their opinion about scientists in an extremely positive way, and over 51 per cent considered their participation in our activities crucial in attracting them towards a scientific career.

As observed by Csermely (2003), attracting young students to scientific research has become a topic of growing importance from the point of view of science and policy-makers. Many scientists, economists and politicians in Europe have been deploring the decreasing numbers of students choosing a career in the sciences and are becoming concerned about a potential lack of scientists and engineers, which could hamper the growth of high-tech industries and the process of social development (Csermely 2003).

The issue of making science and research attractive to young people has sparked many a debate about the future of research and research-related technologies. It has been estimated that Europe needed to attract and train between 600,000 and 700,000 new researchers by 2010 to meet its research needs – a number not yet reached. Last but not least, as science and technology have an increasing influence on individuals and societies, it is equally important for young people to better understand the problems and challenges they create.

We think that activities and events such as the ones we organized may really help make scientific careers attractive for young people. Building capacities and developing innovative ways of connecting science to society is a priority under the EU Framework Programme Horizon 2020. Occasions for younger generations to interact in a friendly way with scientists will help to make science more attractive to young people, increase their appetite for innovation and open up further research and innovation activities.

4.4 Considerations on Science Inspired by our Activities

When respondents were asked to indicate what reflections their participation in the various activities inspired in themselves, they stated that the event showed that "Science improves quality of life" (28 per cent), that "Science needs more equal opportunities" (23 per cent), that "Science is a life opportunity for young people" (18 per cent) and that "Scientists are ordinary people who can achieve extraordinary results for the collective growth" (14 per cent), proving they had at least in part understood that research work is not only for geniuses, but also for those who are passionate and want to contribute through scientific research to the collective growth and well-being.

Even those who have a lower level of education showed they had a general awareness of the importance of research work for young people, as well as for the need for more equal opportunities, especially for girls, as shown in Graph 4.

Overall, a very positive judgement of the event emerges from the survey. In fact, 60 per cent of the respondents assessed the event as one of good quality and almost 19 per cent of the interviewees declared it to be excellent. In particular, visitors liked the interaction with researchers. This is a good result, as it is a clear indication that the possibility to interact in a friendly way with scientists is the most attractive factor of any science outreach activity. We have certainly achieved the objective of raising people's interest and built an attractive space to which people would like to come back.

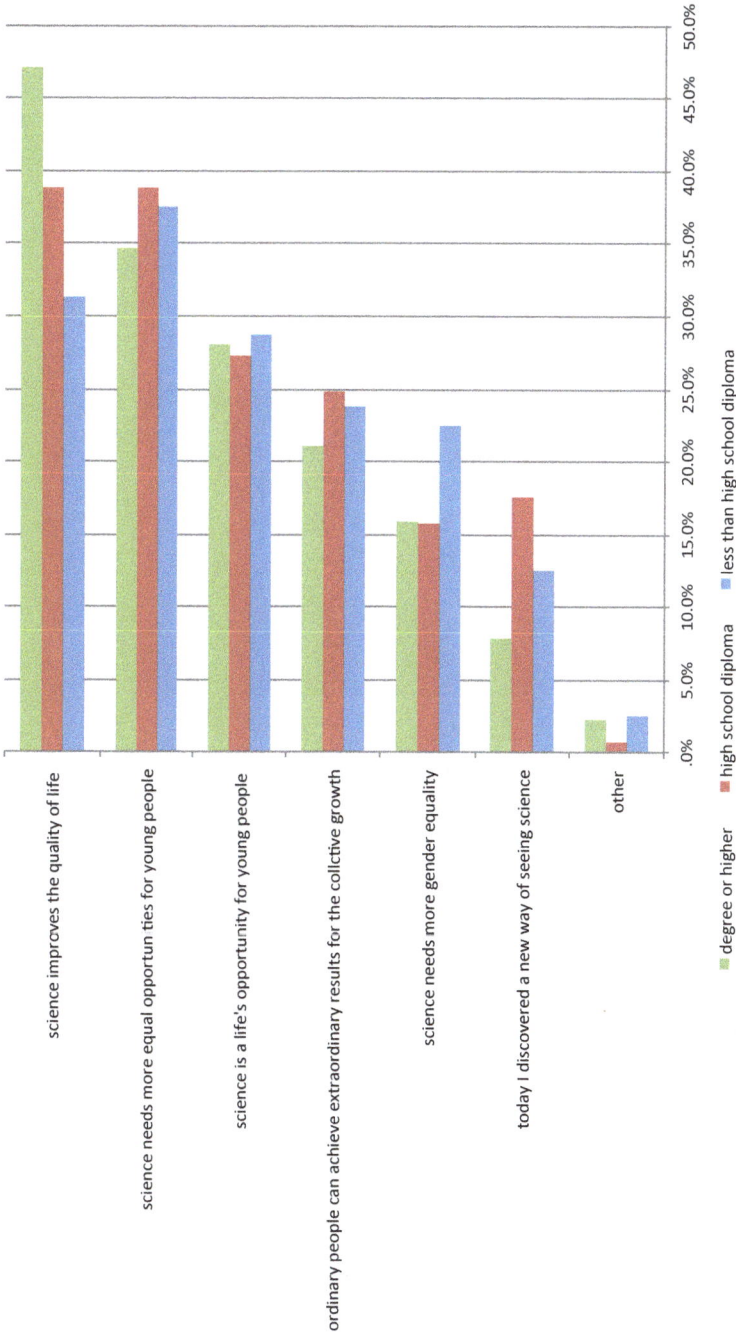

Graph 4. Life opportunity statements about science inspired by our activities (percentages by education).

The general public participating in scientific events may become more knowledgeable and diverse year after year. Our experience demonstrates that a good outreach event needs to be accessible to people from all walks of life, and should aim to make science attractive. This is the reason why we think that our activity is fully appropriate to give scientists and their work status and recognition and has certainly contributed to create a new and more positive image of scientists.

4.5 Lessons Learned and Improvements for the Future

The participation in events aiming to break down stereotypes about science and scientists can generate positive and lasting effects in the medium and long term. Specific actions can make the general public able to digest new information and can make the public start to assess science and scientists in a different way, and to identify more quickly the social impact and everyday-life benefits of scientific progress, and the importance of supporting scientific research and careers. It is likely that the impact of the learning increases in proportion to the duration and intensity of the stimulus or event. The duration of the interaction between researchers and citizens supports the effectiveness of the event and the learning of a new, non-stereotyped cultural form.

Our experience aimed to break down stereotypes about scientists. Therefore, it was essential that scientists abandon their white coats, metaphorically considered as a sign of authority and competency, and present themselves to the public with their passions and their artistic and sporting hobbies, which are part of their everyday life.

An effective science event oriented towards enhancing the image of science should excite audiences and promote gender equal opportunities, community cohesion and cultural exchange, but also develop the scientific pride and the sense of identity of citizens who take part in a positive event for the cultural growth of the community. In this way, people could be stimulated to seek a greater understanding of all forms of science and culture, and to explore new cultural views.

Our survey did not include a follow-up sample. The follow-up is necessary to assess the temporal "reliability" of changes in stereotyping about scientists. We did not have the opportunity to include it due to lack of funding, but were lucky enough to have the possibility to repeat the event once a year for a period of six years. Therefore, on the one hand we had a periodic reinforcement of the positive messages about scientists, and on the other hand we had the possibility to check the change in attitudes towards scientists of those who participated to our activities more than once over time.

For the future, we are planning a "*Light* on tour" event to be held regularly in different cities. This would also certainly lead to a strengthening of the positive image of scientists through the virtuous circle it will create in the media. Being a demographer and a sociologist, our great aspiration is to improve our methodological approach to assess the effects of our activities over time by means of follow-up studies involving the same sample of attendees exposed to activities that aim to de-stereotype scientists. For the moment this remains an elusive goal. A more realistic improvement – though very difficult to implement in practice – may be to interview a sample of attendees both at the entrance and at the exit of the event in order to measure the effect of their exposure to our activities.

To conclude, the following recommendations may be of help when planning the evaluation of large public outreach events:

- understand the motivations and expectations of visitors;
- choose visitor-centred goals that reflect the free-choice nature of these events;
- use data collection tools that allow for easy deployment at a variety of locations.

Did we make a difference?

We hold stereotypes. Everybody does that. For scientists it is a little harder to demonstrate who they simply are, because often people are blind to non-stereotyped views of scientists and science. Some of the elements of the stereotypes concerning scientists, for example the fact that they are smart and hard-working, are certainly true and are in fact important characteristics of a good scientist. But being eccentric and socially isolated and living an unbalanced life are not realistic traits that can be applied to all the members of the scientific community; scientists are normal people with families, friends, hobbies.

The objective of our *Light* project was twofold: first, to foster an enthusiasm for the scientific process of discovery and to promote an interest in future participation in science-related careers for young people; second, to offer people with different cultural backgrounds the opportunity to change their stereotypical ideas of science and scientists. In order to achieve these goals, the activities were centred on the interaction between scientists and citizens: non-scientists used scientific tools, talked with real scientists, and gained scientific knowledge so that they may become informed members of their communities.

What we have done, as compared to other activities aimed at changing people's stereotypical image of scientists, presents points of strength and weaknesses. Hopefully, what we did better than anyone else was to achieve a real interaction between scientists and the public. This was achieved through a purposively designed set-up of the venue of the event, aimed at eliminating potential barriers to effective interaction between scientists and the public. The spatial context has a great impact on verbal and nonverbal communication and on the quality of interaction, although this is often overlooked. Organizers of science communication events take for granted the idea that tables, chairs, microphones, screens etc. are neutral tools, and do not perceive them as elements that create a communication barrier between the experts and the public. In a situation where people were coming to specifically interact with scientists, to be convinced to change their ideas about scientists or to be inspired by science, it was essential to do whatever we could to remove the barriers – literally and figuratively – between experts and laypeople.

We had architects and event designers as our partners for the project. They understood our needs and supported the strategic decisions we took when planning activities aimed at dismantling stereotypes about scientists. From the early stages of the project, architects assessed the venue, set out options, carried out feasibility studies and helped us to develop the project brief into strategic activities.

A good example of this is the glass ceiling sensorial experience described in Chapter 2, which is an effective tool to make people aware of the existence of gender stereotypes in science. We set up the glass ceiling experience in different contexts, for example in one of Rome's biggest shopping centre or next to a modern art museum. These sites did not have any connection with science, so the people passing by did not expect to be confronted with the scientific world: it was amazing to see people queuing to go through the glass ceiling experience, asking questions after having gone through it and showing a clear interest about the situation of female scientists.

We also made efforts to eliminate the language barriers between scientists and ordinary people. We know that the words we choose, how we use them and the meaning we attach to them cause many communication barriers. Furthermore, if people do not understand the words, they cannot understand the message. That is the reason why we strongly recommend to brief scientists who participate in science communication events. We did it, and had very good results in improving the communication skills of scientists.

A further strength of our events to favour the change of people's stereotypical image of scientists was the possibility for the public to see what scientists do when they do not do science through the Globe Science Theatre activity, where scientists performed their hobbies, dancing, playing or doing sport. This was a crucial aspect to show the human side of scientists and to break down psychological barriers between scientists and ordinary people.

To realize all these activities we had the advantage of having unique, low-cost resources at our disposal that others cannot easily obtain: CNR researchers participated at no cost and came from all over the country, the CNR press office was extremely helpful and effective in contacting the media and we had access for free to very costly equipment and to low-cost venues. Last but not least, we had funds from the European Commission.

We are conscious that nothing is perfect and that there are aspects of our activity that should be improved. A weak point of *Light*'s impact assessment was the absence of follow-up data to evaluate the long-term outcomes on people's opinions on scientists. It may be possible to alter negative attitudes towards scientists and science by giving people accurate information and the possibility of interacting with scientists, but the change may be short-lived. If you want to repeat our experience, we suggest you plan a follow-up survey. For us this was impossible due to the extremely high number of participants and the limited budget. However, it was possible to follow-up the younger participants of the INV-Factor competition: more than 70 per cent of the young inventors decided to choose a STEM education – and will hopefully choose a STEM job.

New opportunities are coming to the fore in Europe. As mentioned in the introduction, the European Union has launched a seven-year RRI (Responsible Research and Innovation) strategy. RRI is largely based on "public engagement", which essentially means the involvement of a diversity of stakeholders – representing research, industry, and policy and public bodies, including civil society organizations – and citizens in general. There are plenty of benefits in involving the broadest possible range of actors in innovation and research, but it is essential to remove bias and stereotypes that make the dialogue and interaction between experts and non-experts difficult, if not impossible. Thus, initiatives and actions aimed at removing stereotypes about scientists can be of great help.

Moreover, we live in a period of changes in social patterns, population profiles and lifestyles, of increasing levels of education in the population, increasing attention of people towards scientific progress that makes life better and an increasing interest of governments in encouraging young boys and girls to choose a scientific career. People with increased education levels, knowledge and scientific outlook are more liable to change their points of view, and their stereotypical images of scientists are more easily changed.

But did we really make a difference in changing unrealistic stereotypical images of what a scientist is and does in people's minds? Let us be entirely honest with ourselves and with our readers. Actions aimed at changing stereotypes of scientists are infrequent. When actions are implemented, stereotypes do change with time, but often they only fade and are not totally removed from people's minds. Undoubtedly mass media play an important role in the maintenance of stereotypical images of scientists, as we said in previous chapters. All this lets us conclude that although stereotypes concerning scientists grow weaker when ordinary people are exposed to actions aimed at modifying their clichéd ideas on science and scientists, they often persist. This is not a good reason for doing nothing: it is in fact a good reason to perform counter-stereotypical actions and activities concerning scientists more often.

References

ASPIRES. (2013). *Young people's science and career aspirations, age 10–14. Final Report.* Department of Education & Professional Studies, London: King's College.

Ballantyne, D. (2004). Dialogue and its role in the development of relationship specific knowledge, *Journal of Business and Industrial Marketing,* 19 (2), pp. 114–123.

Bandura, A., Barbaranelli, C., Caprara, G. V., Pastorelli, C. (2001). Self-efficacy beliefs as shapers of children's aspirations and career trajectories. *Child Development, 72,* pp. 187–206.

Blade Runner. (1982) Film. Directed by Ridley Scott. USA: Warner Bros

Bohren, C.F. (2001). *Clouds in a Glass of Beer: Simple Experiments in Atmospheric Physics.* Courier Corporation.

Bones. (2005). H. creator. USA: Fox

Bourdieu, P. (1998). *La domination masculine.* Paris: Seuil.

Brownell, S.E., Price, J.V., and Steinman, L. (2013). Science Communication to the General Public: Why We Need to Teach

Undergraduate and Graduate Students this Skill as Part of Their Formal Scientific Training, *Journal of Undergraduate Neuroscience Education*. Published online, Fall; 12(1).

Bucholtz, M. (1999). "Why be normal?": Language and identity practices in a community of nerd girls, *Language in Society*, 28(02), 203.

Bultitude, K. (2011). The Why and How of Science Communication. In Rosulek, P. (ed.), *Science Communication*. Pilsen: European Commission.

Castell, S., Charlton, A., Clemence, M., Pettigrew, N., Pope, S., Quigley, A., Shah, J. N., and Silman, T. (2014). *Public attitudes to science 2014. Main report*. Ipsos MORI Social Research Institute.

Chambers, D. W. (1983). Stereotypic Images of the Scientist: The Draw-a-Scientist Test, *Science Education*, 67, pp. 255–265.

Correll, S. J. (2004). Constraints into preferences: Gender, status, and emerging career aspirations, *American Sociological Review*, 69 (1), pp. 93–113.

Craik, K. H. (2008). *Reputation: A network interpretation*. New York: Oxford University Press.

Crichton, M. (1990). *Jurassic Park*. New York: Alfred A. Knopf

Crichton, M. (1990). *Jurassic Park*. New York: Alfred A. Knopf publisher.

Criminal Minds. (2005). Davis, J. creator. USA: CBS

Cross, T. L. (2005). Nerds and Geeks: Society's Evolving Stereotypes of Our Students With Gifts and Talents, *Social/Emotional Needs*, 28, 4, pp. 26–28.

Csermely, P. (2003). Recruiting the younger generation to science, *EMBO Reports.*, Sep; 4(9): 825–828.

CSI. (2000). Zuiker, A.E. creator. USA: CBS

Deloitte Consulting (2014). Researchers' Report 2014. Final Report. [Online] Available from: http://ec.europa.eu/euraxess/index.cfm/general/researchPolicies. [Accessed: 20 August 2015].

Dikmenli, M. (2010). Undergraduate biology students' representations of science and the scientist, *College Student Journal*, 44: 579–588.

Dovidio, J. (2009). *Five Questions for John Dovidio, PhD.* American Psychological Association. [Online] Available from: http://www.apa.org/news/press/releases/2009/02/questions-dovidio.aspx. [Accessed: 11 March 2016].

Dr. Strangelove , Or: How I Learned to Stop Worrying and Love the Bomb (1964). Film. Directed by Stanley Kubrick. USA: Columbia Pictures Corporation

Eglash, R. (2002). Race, Sex, and Nerds: from Black Geeks to Asian-Americans Hipsters, *Social Text*, 20 (271), 49–64. [Online] Available from: http://dx.doi.org/10.1215/01642472-20-2_71-49 [Accessed: 11 March 2016].

Eugster, P. (2007). The Perception of Scientists, *The Science Creative Quarterly*. [Online] Available from: https://ec.europa.eu/programmes/horizon2020/en/h2020-section/science-and-society

Eurobarometer (2010). *Special Eurobarometer survey: Science and Technology* Directorate for Communication: Luxembourg.

Eurobarometer (2015). *Public opinion on future innovations, science and technology*. Directorate for Communication: Luxembourg.

European Commission (2001). Eurobarometer 55.2 – Europeans, Science and Technology. *Special Eurobarometer. 340/wave 73.1. TNS Opinion & Social.* Luxembourg: Office for Official Publications of the European Communities.

European Commission (2007a). *Science Education Now: A Renewed Pedagogy for the Future of Europe.* Luxembourg: Office for Official Publications of the European Communities.

European Commission (2007b). Work Programme 2008: People, C (2007) 5740 of 28 November 2007, p. 25.

European Commission (n.d.). *Science with and for society*, available from: https://ec.europa.eu/programmes/horizon2020/en/h2020-section/science-and-society [Accessed: 26 September 2016].

European Parliament (2015). Women's careers in science and universities, and glass ceilings encountered. Report to the Plenary Sitting 20 July. [Online] http://www.europarl.europa.eu/sides/getDoc.do?pubRef. [Accessed: 5th November 2015].

Eurostat (2016). R & D personnel. *Statistics explained.* [Online] Available from: http://ec.europa.eu/eurostat/statistics-explained/index.php/R_%26_D_personnel. [Accessed: 920 November December 20165].

Feliú-Mójer, M. I. (2015). Effective Communication, Better Science, *Scientific American,* February, Available from: http://http://blogs.scientificamerican.com/guest-blog/effective-communication-better-science/ [Accessed: 8 May 2016].

Frayling, C. (2005). Hollywood's Changing Take on the Scientist, *New Scientist,* 2518 (24).

Geoghegan-Quinn, M. (2012). Message delivered at the conference "Science in Dialogue – Towards a European Model for Responsible Research and Innovation". Odense, Denmark, 23–25 April.

Gottfredson, L. S. (1981). Circumscription and compromise: A developmental theory of occupational aspirations [Monograph]. *Journal of Counseling Psychology, 28,* 545–579.

Grand, A. (2012). Reaching Out: The Café Scientifique Movement. [Online] *Soapbox Science Blog,* 31 May. http://blogs.nature.com/soapboxscience/2012/05/31/reaching-out-the-cafe-scientifique-movement. [Accessed: 2 November 2015].

Gravity. (2013). Film. Directed by Alfonso Cuarón. UK/USA: Warner Bros

Haynes, R. D. (2003). From alchemy to artificial intelligence: Stereotypes of the scientist in Western literature, *Public Understanding of Science,* 12 (3), pp. 243–253.

Haynes, R. D. (2014). Whatever happened to the 'mad, bad' scientist? Overturning the stereotype, *Public Understanding of Science,* 25 (1), pp. 31–44.

Hewstone, M. (1994). Revision and change of stereotypic beliefs: In search of the elusive subtyping model. In Stroebe , W. & Hewstone, M. (eds.). *European review of social psychology,* 5, pp. 69–109. Chichester, England: Wiley.

Hilgartner, S. (1990). The Dominant View of Popularization: Conceptual Problems, Political Uses, *Social Studies of Science,* 20, 3: pp. 519–539.

Hodson, G., and Hewstone, M. (2013). *Advances in intergroup contact*. NY: Psychology Press.

House, M.D. (2004). Shore, D. creator. USA: Fox

Jenkinson, A., Sain, B., and Bishop, K. (2005). Optimising communications for charity brand management, *International Journal of Nonprofit and Voluntary Sector Marketing*, 10, pp. 79–92.

Jensen, E. (2014). The problems with science communication evaluation, *International School for Advanced Studies. Journal of Science Communication*.

Joyce, A. and Dzoga, M. (2011). *Science, technology, engineering and mathematics education: overcoming challenges in Europe*, [Online] Available from: http://www.ingenious-science.eu/c/document_library. [Accessed: 21 December 2015]European SchoolNet, Brussels.

Kahneman, D. (2011). *Thinking, Fast and Slow*. New York: Farrar, Straus and Giroux.

Kendall, L. (1999). "The Nerd Within": Mass Media and the Negotiation of Identity Among Computer-Using Men, *The Journal of Men's Studies*, 7 (3), 353–369.

Koolstra, C. M. (2008). An example of a science communication evaluation study: Discovery07, a Dutch science party, *International School for Advanced Studies. Journal of Science Communication*, 7 (2), 1–9.

Leon, A. J. (2014). *The Good, The Geek, and the Ugly: a Critical Examination of the Portrayal of Geek Women in Popular Media*. (Thesis, Lehigh University, Pennsylvania). [Online] http://preserve.lehigh.edu/cgi/viewcontent.cgi?article=2538& context=etd. [Accessed: October 5 2016].

Lippmann, W. (1991). *Public opinion*. New Brunswick and London: Transaction Publishers.

Marnell, G. (2012). The perils of popularising science. *The Huffington Post*. [Online] http://www.huffingtonpost.com/richard/schiffman/rick/santorum/statements_b_1293657.html. [Accessed: March 21 2016].

Martin, B. (1992). Why academic jargon thrives. *The Australian*, 23 September, p. 16.

McClendon, M.J. (1974). Interracial contact and reduction of prejudice. *Social Focus* 7, pp. 47–65.

McConnell, S. (2004). *Professional Software Development: Shorter Schedules, Better Projects, Superior Products, Enhanced Careers.* Boston, MA: Addison-Wesley.

Mead, M., and Métraux, R. (1957). Image of the scientist among high school students: A pilot study. *Science*, 126, pp. 384–390.

Mercier, E. M., Barron, B., and O'Connor, K. M. (2006). Images of self and others as computer users: The role of gender and experience. *Journal of Computer Assisted Learning*, 22, 335–348. [Online] Available from: http://dx.doi:10.1111/j.1365-2729.2006.00182.x. [Accessed: 2 March 2016].

Merton, R. K. (1948). The Self-Fulfilling Prophecy. *The Antioch Review*, 8 (2), pp. 193–210. Available from: http://www.jstor.org/stable/4609267. [Accessed: March 1 2016].

NCIS. (2009). Bellisario, D.P., McGill D. creators. USA: CBS

Ndom, R. J. E., Elegbeleye, A. O., and Williams, A. (2008). The Effect of Stereotype on Cognitive Performance: An Experimental Study of Female Cognitive Performance, *Journal of Gender and Behaviour*, 6 (2), pp. 1793–1809.

Nisbet, M.I., and Dudo, A. (2013). Entertainment Media Portrayals and Their Effects on the Public Understanding of Science, in Hollywood Chemistry, *ACS Symposium Series*, Vol. 1139, Chapter 20, pp. 241–249.

Numbers. (2005). Falacci, N., Heuton, C. creators. USA: CBS

Odifreddi, P. (2012). I pazzi scienziati. *La Repubblica*, 19 luglio.

OECD (2008). *Increasing student interest in S&T studies.* Paris: OECD Publishing.

Palomba, R. (2013). *Sognando Parità.* Milan: Salani Editore.

Palomba, R. (2015). Gender Equality. In Archibugi, D. et al. *The contribution of science and society (FP6) and science and society (FP7) to Responsible Research and Innovation. A Review.* APRE: Rome.

Pink, D.H. (2009). *Drive: The Surprising Truth About Motivating Others.* New York: Riverhead Books, Penguin Group (USA).

Quail, C. (2011). Nerds, Geeks, And The Hip/Square Dialectic In Contemporary Television. *Television & New Media*, 12 (5), 460–482.

Ramirez-Berg, C. (2002). Categorizing the other: Stereotypes and Stereotyping. In Ramirez-Berg, C. *Latino Images in Film: Stereotypes, Subversion, Resistance*, Austin: University of Texas Press.

Ranganathan, J. (2013). Scientists: do outreach or your science dies. *Scientific American*. [Online] 4th June. Available from: http://blogs.scientificamerican.com/guest-blog/scientists-do-outreach-or-your-science-dies/.[Accessed: 2nd November 2015].

Robinson, S. (2014). *Fake geek girl: the gender conflict in nerd culture* (Thesis, Conflict and Dispute Resolution Program, University of Oregon). [Online] Available from: https://scholars bank.uoregon.edu/xmlui/bitstream/handle/1794/18385/ Robinson_oregon_0171N_10998.pdf?sequence=1 [Accessed: 10 March 2016].

Root-Bernstein, R. (2008). Arts Foster Scientific Success: Avocations of Nobel, National Academy, Royal Society, and Sigma Xi Members. *Journal of Psychology of Science and Technology* 1(2):51–63.

Rothbart, M. (1996). Category-exemplar dynamics and stereotype change. *International Journal of Intercultural Relations*. 20, pp. 305–321.

Rothbart, M., and John, O. P. (1985). Social categorization and behavioural episodes: A cognitive analysis of the effects of intergroup contact. *Journal of Social Issues*, 41, pp. 81–104.

Runco, M.A., and Pritzker, S. R. (eds) (1999). *Encyclopedia of creativity*, 1st Ed., London, Burlington, San Diego: Academic Press.

Sardo, M., and Grand, A. (2014). *Evaluation of the wellcome trust strand at the latitude festival 2014*. Project Report. University of the West of England, Bristol, Bristol.

Scheffer, M., Bascompte, J., Bjordam, T. K., Carpenter, S. R., Clarke, L. B., Folke, C., Marquet, P., Mazzeo, N., Meerhoff,

M., Sala, O., and Westley, F. R. (2015). Dual thinking for scientists. *Ecology and Society* 20(2): 3. http://dx.doi.org/10.5751/ES-07434-200203

Schneider, D.J. (2004). *The Psychology of Stereotyping.* New York: The Guilford Press

Shelley, M. *Frankenstein; or, the modern Prometheus.* (1818). London: Lackington, Hughes, Harding, Mavor, & Jones. Translation in Italian by Zanolli, C., Caretti, L. (1982). Milan: Arnoldo Mondadori

Sosnizkij, B. (2003). Stereotypes in Cross Cultural Communication regarding Germans, *GRIN Verlag* (June), Seminar paper.

Star Trek. (2005) Fuller, B., Kurtz man A. creators. USA: CBS

Star Wars. (1977). Film. Directed by George Lucas. USA: Lucasfilm, Twentieth Century Fox Film Corporation

Stebbins, R.A. (2014). *Serious Leisure and Self-Fulfilment.* London: Palgrave Macmillan.

Tajfel, H. (1974). Social Identity and Intergroup Behavior, *Social Science Information*, April, 13, pp. 65–93.

The Martian. (2015). Film. Directed by Ridley Scott. USA: 20th Century Fox

Tintori, A. (2013). Sebben che siamo donne… ? In Avveduto, S. (ed), *Saperi in rete. Scenari e prospettive su popolazione, welfare, scienza e società*, Rome: CNR-Irpps, pp. 99–109.

Tintori, A. (2015). *Scenari futuri e giudizio informato. Un innovativo metodo Delphi*, Rome: Aracne Editrice .

Tocci, J. (2007). *The well-dressed geek: media appropriation and subcultural style.* MiT5. Lecture conducted from Massachusetts Institute of Technology, Philadelphia. [Online] http://web.mit.edu/comm-forum/mit5/papers/Tocci.pdf. [Accessed: 25 February 2016].

Turney, J.(1998). *Frankenstein's Footsteps: Science, Genetics and Popular Culture.* London: Yale University Press

Valente, A. (2015). Science Education. In Archibugi, D. et al. *The contribution of science and society (FP6) and science and society (FP7) to Responsible Research and Innovation. A Review.* CNR edizioni: Rome.

van Tuij C ., Walma van der Molen, J. H. 2016. Study choice and career development in STEM fields: an overview and integration of the research, *International Journal of Technology and Design education* 26, 2, May, pp :159–183

Wells, H.G. (1896). *The Island of Doctor Moreau.* London: Heinemann, Stone & Kimball

Woo, B. (2012). Alpha nerds: Cultural intermediaries in a subcultural scene. *European Journal of Cultural Studies, 15(5),* 659–676.

Woolston, C. (2015). Leisure activities: The power of a pastime. *Nature,* 523, pp. 117–119.